Elena Ferrante's *The Neapolitan Novels*

BOOKMARKED

Elena Ferrante's

The Neapolitan Novels

BOOKMARKED

GINA FRANGELLO

New York, NY

Printed in the United States of America.

This book is memoir. It reflects the author's present recollections of experiences over time. Some names and characteristics have been changed, some events have been compressed, and some dialogue has been recreated

Ig Publishing
Box 2547
New York, NY 10163
www.igpub.com

ISBN: 978-1-63246-162-9

For the girls and women of my Old Neighborhood. Those who left, those who stayed, and those eternally poised between.

INTRODUCTION[1]

To say that I have a few autobiographical similarities to the narrator of Elena Ferrante's *My Brilliant Friend*—a single novel in four installments often referred to in English as "The Neapolitan Novels" or the Neapolitan "Quartet"—would be a vast understatement. Like the narrator of all four volumes, Elena ("Lenu") Greco, I was also born into a close-knit yet violent Italian neighborhood that no one ever seemed to leave, and, like Lenu, I fantasized constantly about "getting out," using education as my primary propeller toward a different fate. Like Lenu, I became a writer, married a brainy introvert from a more educated family, raised children, struggled with the dichotomies between family life and making art, had a passionate affair, found myself constantly

1. Thanks to *Electric Literature*, where a variation on parts of this introduction originally appeared as "What We Talk About When We Talk About Elena Ferrante."

returning to the city I'd once sworn to escape, ultimately left my marriage, and struggled with the challenges of making a living as a writer while parenting three children.

Most significantly, as it is the heart of the Neapolitan Novels, my youth was also marked indelibly by my intimacy with a more beautiful, more charismatic and powerful girl who, despite her many gifts, seemed doomed. In Ferrante's novels, this is the character of Raffaella Cerullo, called "Lina" by everyone but the narrator, who calls her only Lila. In my own memoir, *Blow Your House Down: A Story of Family, Feminism, and Treason*, I dubbed this friend "Angie," a composite character streamlined both for narrative clarity and to protect privacy. In this text, I will therefore continue to refer to that childhood friend as Angie, in part for consistency, and also because—as with the alliteration of Lenu and Lila—the other intimate girlhood/lifelong friend I'll discuss in this book is called Alyssa (not her real name). Many of the dynamics between Lenu and Lila were also replicated in *that* friendship, only in a less dichotomous or binary way . . . which is to say that with Alyssa, sometimes I found myself the Lila, and sometimes the Lenu, over the duration of a bond that has now lasted for forty-five years. Life, unlike literature, does not often distill cleanly to one relationship through which every possible interpersonal dynamic is played out (one reason composite characters are so common, aside from privacy issues, in memoir), and so for me, Angie and Alyssa together embody in my own life the Lenu-Lila dynamic.

Of course, Ferrante writes of girlhood in 1950s Naples (Lenu and Lila are both born in August of 1944), whereas Alyssa, Angie, and I were all born in 1968 and came of age in Chicago in the 1970s and 80s. The turbulent political landscape of Italy during some sixty years covered by Ferrante's four novels is divergent in many ways from the (also turbulent) history of the United States, and the quintessential *Italianness* of the Neapolitan Novels is integral to the fate of its characters and radically different from my experience of Italian *Americanness.* Whereas in my old neighborhood, boys growing to men in a state of hopeless poverty and stagnation often turned to gangs or became small-time workers for the Mob, those in Lenu and Lila's world are as likely to become involved with Communism or Fascism, go on the run for political crimes, or attend political meetings in secret, as they are to become "gangsters"—in fact, the two things seem somewhat inextricable, especially with regards to organized crime in the United States, where politics and the Mafia have tended to be financial bedfellows but less associated with the exact same actors, especially among the working class.[2]

Ferrante's novels' immersion in Italy—in particular Naples, and more specifically one poor, dialect-infused neighborhood in the city—is crucial to the understanding of how intensely personal readers' responses to Ferrante have tended to be. Because although I am Italian American and grew up below the poverty line in a neighborhood quite similar to Lenu's and Lila's, that fact—or any other biographical fact—seems irrelevant when considering that almost every woman reader gripped by so-called "Ferrante

---

2. The exception to this, in my old neighborhood and in the city of Chicago in general, especially in that era, was the role "Aldermen" played in neighborhood politics. Make no mistake: someone would need to have just arrived from Mars to make the argument that Chicago politics were not largely intertwined with organized crime, and it was the norm in my neighborhood and many others for most locals to vote in elections the way the Alderman instructed them to do, and common colloquial knowledge that many Aldermen had connections with organized crime. But as I was only a child and—like Lenu—left my old neighborhood for college, and unlike Lenu, although I returned to Chicago eventually as she does to Naples, I never again lived in the confines of my old neighborhood, so I cannot pretend to be as knowledgeable about the inner workings of the Chicago political machine as it intersected with the so-called Chicago Outfit. This being said, it is certainly true that exactly zero teens I ever knew in my old neighborhood were obsessed with large ideological concepts such as Communism, Fascism, or for that matter Democracy, so where politics and organized crime—and possibly gangs—intersected seems to have been the terrain of adults.

fever" seems to feel similarly: as though these books were written *for her, to her*, revealing the insides of her own messy guts and brain. As Claire Messud wrote in an email to Meghan O'Rourke, when O'Rourke was writing about Ferrante for *The Guardian*, "When you write to me and say you love her work, I have a moment where I think, 'But . . . Elena is my friend! My private relationship with her, so intense and so true, is one that nobody else can fully know!'"[i] To love Ferrante, especially in the days prior to her work being widely made into television series, was almost akin to a secret handshake in certain bookish, feminist circles. Yet it is fair to extrapolate that most of her avid American fans had upbringings radically different from Lenu's and Lila's in Naples. What readers relate to most are her characters' fearlessly naked, almost unfathomably nuanced interior lives and relationships. You don't have to be Italian, or poor, or have a "getting out" story, or to have known anyone in organized crime, to feel that Ferrante's novels cut closer to the bone than other works of fiction.

This reputation—built long before her books were being made into media series' and she was an international name—was built largely on word-of-mouth buzz. Ferrante had already become Italy's best-known writer in English even though nobody knew the actual identity of the pseudonymous author. In our era of social media accessibility, influencer culture, self-promotion, and an obsession with hot young celebrities, this is nothing short of astounding: an unseen Italian woman of a certain age, of whom the critic James Wood wrote, "[c]ompared with Ferrante, Thomas Pynchon is a publicity profligate," managed to make droves of readers worldwide feel the way one feels when a favorite indie band signs on a major label: *wait, that's my band—they were writing about and singing for me!*[ii]

If it was once difficult to talk about Ferrante without directly discussing gender and authorship, after 2016 it became impossible.[3] But eschewing questions of Ferrante's identity for the moment and focusing on her readership, if one goes by anecdotal and critical evidence her audience is predominantly female, and even male critics who laud her see her work as highly gendered. Writes Wood, "Ferrante may never mention Hélène Cixous or French feminist

3. In 2016, Elena Ferrante was "outed" by Claudio Gatti as the translator Anita Raja, born in Naples as the well-off daughter of a magistrate and married to the prize-winning Italian novelist Dominico Starnone; in 2021, the tables turned when computer analysis pronounced Starnone to be the "real" author of the novels. Both "revelations" were greeted predominantly with indignation by Ferrante fans, who approved of her wish to write pseudonymously, and who, later, seemed so agitated by the possibility that Ferrante could be a man that the discussion all but died out entirely following Starnone-gate.

literary theory, but her fiction is a kind of practical *écriture feminine*."[iii] One certainly doesn't have to be a woman to appreciate Ferrante . . . but to what extent might being one change the experience? When I was halfway through the inaugural novel in the series, *My Brilliant Friend*, in the twilight of 2014, I posted on Facebook that the book should be "required reading for anyone who wants to understand female psychology." A decade later, I still relate to that sentiment, but at the same time have grown wary of my own description. "Nothing quite like it has ever been published," writes Meghan O'Rourke of the series in *The Guardian*: "four novels that make up a single book . . . a kind of quasi-feminist *bildungsroman* that also happens to be a history of Italy in the late 20th century."[iv] What is clear is that these novels are profoundly ambitious literary feats, unique in tone, style, and scope, when it often seems everything has already been done. Ferrante's achievement—one novel, told in four luminous volumes—manages to be written with a complete absence of what Claire Vaye Watkins dubbed as "pandering"[4] to the male literary establishment. If anything is clear from Lenu's voice—from Ferrante's writing across *all* her books—it is that she implicitly writes for the universal

---

4. See Vaye Watkins' seminal 2015 piece, "On Pandering," in *Tin House*: https://tinhouse.com/on-pandering.

She. Her prose—passionate, intimate, urgent, confiding—show no aesthetic concern for courting either male literary traditions or, perhaps, even male readers as a means of legitimizing her art; indeed, she hasn't "needed" them. (Still, she is so scarily good that I can't help but wonder: why doesn't she have more of them *anyway*?)

Critics are not much divided on Ferrante in terms of acclaim for her writing, but are quite divided—and at times downright *odd*—in their discussion of *why*, in ways that also circle issues of gender. The Neapolitan Novels, arguably the deepest, widest and richest portrait of a lifelong friendship between two girls/women ever documented in literature (Ferrante often draws comparisons to Lessing in this regard, but the depth of her exploration of Lenu and Lila, over four books, truly has no rival), is a complicated artistic beast to be sure, yet the core focus on female friendship has tended to cause some critics to treat the novel's complexity and multiplicity as so genre-busting and defying of categorization that it can smack of patronizing cloaked in praise. Writes Elizabeth Lowry in the *Wall Street Journal*: "How should we classify Elena Ferrante's magnificently complicated Neapolitan quartet? The three previous titles in the series—*My Brilliant Friend* (2012), *The Story of a New Name* (2013) and *Those Who Leave and Those*

Who Stay (2014)—defy categorization. Are they genre or literary fiction? Soap operas? Political epics? Some form of memoir?"[v] Though it is not in itself in any way an "insult" to have one's novel seen as multidimensional or nonconforming to one specific literary genre, it's also impossible not to question whether a series of novels that explored the *male* psyche and relationships between men, while also involving politics, class issues, and a certain amount of meta exploration of literature itself, would be described as though its diverse themes were… so surprising as to defy categorization. Didn't Updike attempt something similar in his Rabbit series, and Roth through Zuckerman, and Elroy in his Los Angeles Quartet? Is serious fiction that chronicles characters over time and explores both the innermost depths of their intimate relationships, along with the political climate of the times and a profound interrogation of class struggles, truly such a confounding thing as to call into question whether we are reading a *soap opera*, or, as Lowry later invokes in her review, a thriller? Or does it only *seem* so because the focal characters are girls/young women for most of the pages?

If the lives of girls and young women are too often trivialized by the literary establishment (in the United States and in Europe), they are treated with mythical devotion by

Ferrante. Indeed, one weakness of the Neapolitan Novels may be that Ferrante devotes so little page time to Lenu and Lila as mature women, in fact titling the final section of the novel, which focuses on the characters' lives between the ages of forty to sixty-six—brace yourself—"Old Age." The singularly defining event of their lives (Ferrante's titles are full of spoilers and this text will also include many) occurs in the final novel when Lenu and Lila have just turned forty and Lila's beloved daughter Tina goes (permanently) missing under mysterious circumstances never revealed. The rest of their lives, especially once past fifty, are then sped over in strokes so broad as to be positively un-Ferrantean and that seem to reinforce patriarchal stereotypes of women becoming invisible with age. Here is a writer who can spend an entire thick novel on every thought and deed of girls between the ages of six and sixteen, yet the same women, once menopausal, no longer seem to interest their author much.[5]

Lenu's lovers, as she ages, seem to merit no scenes; if she has close friends after she and Lila part ways, we don't ever meet them. Perhaps Ferrante initially gave herself free

5. Likewise, Lenu's daughters—three women with their own complicated history—are painted with none of the intricacy of the dozens of characters in her old neighborhood, and never rise above "types."

reign and then, after some 1,000 pages, panicked and felt she[6] had better wrap things up already? Whatever the reason, the final third of the final novel feels that thing one never feels when reading a Ferrante novel: rushed. While the first three books—and *The Story of the Lost Child* as well—have a quality of breathless emotional fervor, they also unapologetically languish on any detail or side plot that strikes the narrator's fancy. Guns are delightfully introduced in Act I that are not fired by Act III—people drop away, major concerns shift. Ferrante's Neapolitan Novels, though full of returning characters and at times coincidences that strain at realism, follow the rhythms of a *life* more than a traditional fictional narrative arc. It is disappointing, therefore, when this author who specializes in reading women's minds and hearts seems to indicate that said minds and hearts are inherently less engaging in

---

6. As is likely already clear, Ferrante will be referred to as "she" throughout this exploration, despite controversies of identity linking her to Starnone; in keeping with the metafictional vibes of the Neapolitan Novels, it is clear that Elena Ferrante—no matter the actual identity of her creator—is a female persona, one whose first name corresponds with that of Elena ("Lenu") Greco, the books' narrator—and that in the many layers of authorship built into these texts, "Elena Ferrante," who gives interviews and publishes her letters, is more than just a pseudonym but a fully fleshed alter ego and personality who has been increasingly public over time, and that personality is distinctly female.

advanced age.

Of course, it is arguable that Lenu's story simply becomes less relevant once she "gets out"—something it takes her until her fifties to fully do. Because as much as Lenu's and Lila's stories excavate iconic themes of womanhood, the Neapolitan series is also a quintessential rags-to-riches story, in which the two girls' different ascents from abject poverty, and the intimate-yet-abhorrent neighborhood that keeps its claws in them, are as crucial to the story as any feminist themes or as the characters' elaborate personal lives. Ironically, a piece on *Buzzfeed* held Ferrante up as a great writer of The American Dream. Writes Alissa Quart:

> Where is the American equivalent of Ferrante? . . . The inequality novel that Americans will read in droves, that critics pay attention to? There was once *The Great Gatsby*, Bellow's *Augie March*, Dreiser's *Sister Carrie* and *The Financier*, even Raymond Carver's working-class silent men of 30 years ago. Certainly those who claim the neorealist caption—Jonathan Franzen, recently dubbed an author of 'failed-marriage razzmatazz' by one critic—have neglected this story.[vi]

Though the claim that no American authors are writing novels interrogating social class and either upward or downward mobility seems unfounded,[7] Ferrante's prowess as a chronicler of class, place, and history are not to be overshadowed by her focus on female friendship and motherhood. In the end, however, no single "topic" can fully explain Ferrante's resonance. As Claire Messud writes:

> Politics and feminism are compelling and important subjects but they won't make readers long for the novels with the zeal of a nine-year-old. Only the human heart can do that, the emotionally truthful depiction of the complex web of love, desire, loathing, envy, compassion and pain that binds people over a lifetime. Ultimately, Ferrante has framed her magnum opus—for all its tremendous ambition, and in spite of the tumult of events that resounds through the pages at ever-greater, eventually exhausting, speed—as a simple

7. It also seems oblivious to the factions of the literary establishment who are people of color or immigrants, where I would argue that the tendency to just give novelistic characters mysterious sources of disposable income and no apparent job despite their beautiful lakeside homes, Manhattan apartments, and endless leisure time, are far less common tropes than among white American writers.

> love story. These books deal above all with the perpetually unrequited but never extinguished Platonic passion[8] . . . [vii]

I would extend this further to say that Lenu and Lila's relationship, though central, is not the only uncannily rich relationship propelling the books, and that *character*—characters in interaction with one another and, of course, with themselves—is Ferrante's rarest of gifts. She seems capable of transmitting the untranslatable alchemy of human psychology onto the page in a whole other league from even other contemporary masters of character like Franzen. Accordingly, her audience identifies fiercely with what her characters feel about motherhood, ambition, jealousy, desire, justice, writing, aging. Ferrante writes so ferociously, so from the inside out, that we know the inhabitants of Lenu's world more intricately than we could likely hope to know such a large ensemble cast in even our

8. I'm not entirely certain I agree with Messud on the "unrequited" or the "Platonic" to a complete degree, but for the sake of shorthand it does seem that Lila and Lenu's mutual love for one another rarely reaches a place of joy and seems to feel, to each of them, unbalanced or unequal, and it is also true that the two never engage in a sexual encounter and that both characters would consider their relationship to be Platonic.

own lives[9]. It is easy to emerge from the Neapolitan Quartet feeling slightly dazed, as though everything we have ever heard about "character development" was little more than a bullet point list in the hands of other writers.

And Lila, of course, is both Ferrante's and Lenu's piece de resistance. As Lenu says of her friend, in a cross between rhapsody and lament:

> She possessed intelligence and didn't put it to use but, rather, wasted it, like a great lady for whom all the riches of the world are merely a sign of vulgarity. She stood out among so many because

9. One reason for this—be it a strength or a weakness—is that Ferrante's characters, much like inhabitants of a small and isolated town, seem to solidify by their teens and rarely change significantly in their essence beyond that, including rarely letting go of childhood allegiances unless in a highly dramatic, fractious way. As my own two closest friends—Alyssa and Hector—now more surrogate siblings to me than simply "friends," are both from my old neighborhood and have been my friends since 5th grade, and as—in the 1950s and 60s—leaving the neighborhood was unheard of and most people were born there, married there, raised children there, and died there, I can relate to this impulse in Ferrante's writing, to the implicit implication that no one outside the neighborhood will ever be quite as important to Lenu or Lila as those "from" that place. That being said, Ferrante seems to have reasons beyond the kind of isolationism that exists in both small towns and very poor urban areas, which I will look at more closely in the chapter on "The Beloved Character."

> she, naturally, did not submit to any training, to any use, or to any purpose. All of us had submitted and that submission had—through trials, failures, successes—reduced us. Only Lila, nothing and no one seemed to reduce her.

One fascinating—yet easy to forget at times, in the thousands of pages of writing—aspect of the Neapolitan Novels is the metafictional fact that *Lenu is physically writing them* on her computer as we read, as a "memoir" of her friendship with Lila. As such, we are not only reading about Lila through Lenu's highly biased eyes, but also through the lens of a woman who has just realized that the most important figure in her life has gone missing, and who is therefore—although she refuses to show it to Lila's grown son or even to herself—in a heightened emotional state. The circumstances unfolding as Lenu writes set her up as an unreliable narrator, and—especially on subsequent readings—many of Lenu's assessments of both herself and Lila feel (intentionally, on the part of Ferrante) biased and not necessarily how the reader might interpret them.

In my own experience of first reading the books, I found myself initially taking Lenu's word for things, then—on subsequent readings—becoming irritated with her for the way she frequently misreads and misunderstands people, herself included. Finally, as I revisited the novels again for this project, I came full circle to a kind of wild pleasure that Lenu cannot get outside her own head and experience when writing her story because—come on!—who can? Yes, perhaps time and distance leads to a more objective memoir than writing one in the throes of a mysterious tragedy such as the complete disappearance of a sixty-six-year-old woman . . . but these books, already more nuanced than even most of the great novels, become even more so when we keep in mind that our "author" is our narrator and protagonist.

It is through Lenu's eyes, therefore, that we witness Lila's life, and the reader must hold in her mind not only what we are told about Lila—and indeed "shown" in ways Lenu chooses (or, were she a real person, we would say "the way she remembers events")—but that we must constantly hold Lenu's interpretation as suspect, given what we understand about memory, about rejection, about envy, about love. Can one write a memoir about their friendship with someone of whom they were in turns worshipful, ferally jealous, determined to save, even more determined to surpass, likely in love with, and at times hateful about? Well, certainly one can, and many real and fictional memoirs *have* done so. But should the reader believe that narrator's truth as the only

Truth? When are opinions Ferrante's, vs. when are they "Lenu's," constructed volitionally by Ferrante to make Lenu unreliable in the classic sense: revealing things at every turn that are not always quite what she *thinks* she is revealing?

In our now-memoir-savvy world, most would concur that we are to draw our own conclusions and that any narrator's opinions (certainly one in a metafictional novel posing as memoir) are more like breadcrumbs. Lila, though possibly still alive, is in absentia by her own choice and cannot tell her side of the story. Lenu, on the other hand, hopes to goad her friend back into existence by documenting their friendship, the one thing she swore to Lila she would never do. She looks for traces of Lila in her computer files, living with the fantasy that her friend is so larger than life that she has not only managed to evaporate without a trace but will then find a way—from her hidden location—to hack into Lenu's computer, somehow divining that this memoir is being written, and change it, alter it, collaborate in its creation, as the two talked about co-writing a book as girls. We are told near the end that Lenu has desperately read and reread, looking for traces of Lila, but has not found her; the memoir is complete, Lenu its only author. And so, we should be wary of the interpretations of a woman not only driven by grief but staging a literal *provocation* to anger

Lila out of hiding.

Ironically, when reading a "novel" without such a meta component, there is the option of assuming what we are told happened and who characters are shown to be is "unbiased" (even though of course every author is biased, as every *person* is biased), but there is no such option in the Neapolitan Novels. Despite the mirrored first name—Elena/Elena—Ferrante did not choose to give Elena "Lenu" Greco the Ferrante surname, and so we walk a tightrope between the works as a long four-volume novel by the invisible yet famous novelist Elena Ferrante, and the work as a memoir written over a matter of weeks in the thrall of pain and nostalgia by the character Elena "Lenu" Greco. One writes under an alias; one is suffering immensely . . . believe them completely at your own risk?

For example, was Lila, as in Lenu's estimation, genuinely incapable of being reduced? One can easily imagine Lila laughing at the notion, arguing convincingly that her entire *life* has been a reduction, until she finally reduced to nothing at all, while Lenu has expanded, broken out, soared. *She says/she says.* The Lila of the page—who is both one of the most multidimensional characters in literature, yet also a metaphor, a riddle, a philosophical question with no answer—can never just resolve. "A hallmark of

Ferrante's writing," O'Rourke says in *The Guardian*, "is [this] juxtaposition between matter-of-factness and metaphor, between hyperrealism and hallucinatory distortion." Such is the magic of Lila, of Lenu's memory, and of the series.

In my own life, neither Angie nor Alyssa disappeared without a trace (we are all in our mid-fifties, so theoretically, there's time!), leaving a wake of mystery behind, rendering themselves forever my obsession.

Rather, Angie settled down, got a job, a partner, a dog (in other words, in Lenu's judgmental eyes, she was "reduced"), and although we still keep in touch and I will always love her with a unique intensity, in modern parlance we have long since "grown apart," our lives diverging in very different directions, as these things go. Perhaps, even, there is an element—as there often is—of neither of us quite *wanting* the other around all the time, reminding us both of who we used to be, of the embarrassments and traumas of our youths, the pain we mutually lived in that—at the time—we did not quite recognize as pain because we had never known anything different, and of the envy we each had of the other, which shames me in particular now that I am able to look at Angie's life from an adult lens and recognize it—similarly to Lila's compared with Lenu's—as having been far more brutal and high stakes than my own. Unlike Lenu, who never emerges from her Lila-envy no matter what tragedies befall her friend, I am now rather ashamed of myself for having been jealous of a young girl who was treated poorly in myriad complex ways by her father and was often targeted by older boys for her beauty and grew up far too fast and not in keeping with her own intrinsic desires, whereas my own parents were gentle people and—though it pained me at the time—most of the guys in our neighborhood left me alone due to some combination of my naked antipathy toward them, my mother's overprotectiveness, and my lesser good looks. Angie's life has turned out quite well in the long run, but as with Lila's, it did not look for a long while as though it would play that way, and the fact that it did was absolutely no thanks to me, as I was rushing around the world for school and love and ambition.

Alyssa, on the other hand, is now a teacher in our former elementary school, and continues to be a figure of near daily prominence in my life. She lives only a few blocks from me, with her husband to whom I introduced her, one of their grown daughters, and two highly ill-behaved dogs. She and I went to college in tandem, raised our children in tandem, call ourselves sisters, which defines our relationship better than "best friends," especially given that we are both highly aware that if we met *now*, we would be unlikely to take much notice of each other at all as a potential friend and confidante. We are incredibly different people, one case-in-point being that, like Lila, Alyssa has never lived outside of Chicago. Though we live roughly four miles north of our old neighborhood (a different universe), Alyssa continues to commute daily to our old elementary school to work, and by thirty or so she had settled into a contented middle age, dressing in sensible teacher garb, eschewing makeup, comfortably putting on weight and giving no fucks about it, taking the occasional trip to visit family and never leaving the country, and not taking *any* trip without her daughters and husband until her children were both over eighteen. She was the one "Who Stayed," and I the one "Who Leaves," per the title of Ferrante's second installment, *Those Who Leave and Those Who Stay.*

Um . . . or kind of. Like Lenu, I went away to college and for some time never looked back. I studied and worked in London, traveled Europe, met my first husband (also an American) in France, moved with him to the east coast of the US where we both attended graduate school, came back to Chicago for a while but then was off again to live in Amsterdam, in Switzerland, before finally returning to Chicago in 1999 when, far from the wandering bohemian life I had once aspired to, my aging parents moved into the downstairs apartment of the house I still live in, where they remained until their deaths a few years ago. In that house, my ex and I adopted two daughters and had a third child in an unexpected pregnancy. By the time my debut novel came out at the end of 2005, I had two kindergarten-aged children, two disabled parents who relied on me for much of their daily upkeep and was seven months pregnant. Some "those who leave" I turned out to be!

At the time of this writing, I have lived in Chicago, and specifically in the same home, for twenty-four years. Although I have been far more prone to dash around the country for my work or to take international holidays than Alyssa, for all intents and purposes by this age we might both be Stayers. Angie, too, lives in Chicago, and to my knowledge has never lived anywhere else. In 2017, my second husband, Rob, moved from the Los Angeles area to live with me and my children, as despite my oft-voiced desire to "get out," by then my children were deeply entrenched in lives of their own, my mother growing ever frailer after my father's death. Leaving no longer seemed an option.

Lenu finally leaves Naples for good in 1995, when she is fifty-one. As we speak, Rob and I plan to leave Chicago in September 2024 after our youngest leaves for college;

I will be fifty-six. But even then, I suspect I will be back. For all my travels, Chicago holds my most longstanding friendships, my children's histories and relationships, my beloved writing group. Though in my current life, in which most of my friends are not Italian-American and grew up with college-educated parents, it is incredibly common to have left home by the age of eighteen and to have never returned for more than a summer break at most; for me, such an uprooted way of life, entirely ordinary in the United States, seems unfeasible. We have all—Alyssa, Angie, and I—been marked by the insular and almost feudal nature of our old Italian/Puerto Rican neighborhood, even if we no longer live within its confines.

When I read the Neapolitan Novels, I see my past—at times dizzyingly, uncomfortably, triggeringly; at other times beautifully and affirmingly—but I no longer see *myself*. I am now an age beyond Ferrante's (and Lenu's) interest, relegated to the domain of fading "Old Age," even if, in the life I lead as a contemporary American woman, such invisibility and obscurity is not my actual experience. It is a challenge to love novels this passionately that seem to affirm the erasure of women over fifty, to be mindful of contextualizing them in their era and geography, to understand the erasure of my current life story from a series that (with some notable exceptions) appears to otherwise all but chronicle my life story through my forties. The endeavor requires holding in my mind that it is not the job of a novel to present a utopian vision, but rather to present facts as they seem to the novelist, and even here in the United States in 2024, it is hard to so much as check Facebook without finding some kind of reference to female invisibility post-forty and especially post-menopause. Individual people do not always reflect perfectly larger cultural phenomenon, but just because we may have escaped certain fates (for now) does not mean these fates don't echo the realities of many women's lives.

To love a certain piece of literature—to identify intensely with it—is not the same thing as agreeing with its every implicit bias or viewpoint, and if literature is, in a sense, my church, I come to it with the sensibility that to interrogate and sometimes rail against faith is a duty of the faithful. In this spirit, I come to the *My Brilliant Friend* saga not only to praise and fawn, but to interrogate and dissent. To commit to reading the Neapolitan Novels to begin with is a rigorous and impassioned endeavor, not for every reader. For those who don't go in for digressions, who don't care for the distinction between live-wire emotional prose vs. sentimentality, who cannot be persuaded to care about the lives of young girls no matter how artfully and intelligently presented, the books would be an exercise in frustration, sure to be thrown across the room (where, heavy as they are, something would be broken, just as Lila might desire). For readers willing to be seduced, however, these four intoxicating volumes comprise nothing less than a singular masterpiece. And it is to you—those readers—to whom I now writing, and whom I invite to wade into the muck with me.

ONE

Female Friendship: Envy, Eroticism, and Symbiosis

Of all the material in the Neapolitan Novels, they are by far most widely known for being an intimate sixty-year-saga of an intense, competitive, lifesaving, intellectual, contentious, primary friendship that each of the protagonists, Lenu and Lila, place as a central priority in their lives long after outside factors such as Lenu's pursuit of education and Lila's early marriage, as well as geographical distance,fff would seem to have driven them apart. In a world with no cell phones or internet—in fact, Lenu's home with her parents has no phone and she needs to go out to a local business to make calls—Lenu and Lila remain symbiotic symbols to one another even in the absence of Lila's willingness to write a letter or answer an email.[10]

10. Throughout the four installments of the novel, Lenu writes to Lila repeatedly—at times daily such as when she is on Ischia for a summer—whereas Lila replies only one time, at the age

Female friendship is not as underrepresented as it used to be in fiction when Doris Lessing broke ground by taking it seriously as a subject. From Margaret Atwood's *Cat's Eye* to Toni Morrion's *Sula* to Joanna Rakoff's *A Fortunate Age* to Amy Tan's *The Joy Luck Club* to Liane Moriarty's *Big Little Lies* to Sally Rooney's *Conversations with Friends*—to list only a very few—female friendship has become a hot literary sub-genre. Few books, however, grant the mythic primacy to early girlhood that Ferrante does. "Coming of age" novels about young girls have never quite attained the "universality" ascribed to coming of age novels about boys, written by men, and are often sexistly seen as "niche" in the publishing industry. Ferrante breaks that wide open by devoting the entirety of *My Brilliant Friend*, the first volume

---

of fifteen, and never writes Lenu again despite their friendship lasting for more than half a century. While Lila does not exceed a fifth grade education, she is self-taught and, according to Lenu's narration, an extraordinarily gifted writer whose skills put Lenu's to shame despite her higher education and—later—her becoming a professional writer. Lila also writes a ten-page story, "The Blue Fairy," and fills numerous notebooks keeping a journal. Hence, the reader is definitely not meant to assume that any lack of literary skill prevents Lila from writing letters or emails. Rather, it is a combination of Lila's desire not to discuss the ugliness of her life and the belief that it is not worthy fodder for writing, her unequal power dynamic with Lenu in which she perpetually keeps Lenu wanting more than she receives, and Lila's lifelong desire to "erase herself," which she achieves totally at the age of sixty-six.

in the quartet, to the ages of six to sixteen, audaciously constructing it so epically and with such literary chops that it in no way conforms to industry expectations around many novels about girlhood—as a "YA novel," "beach book," "chick lit," or even "women's fiction"[11]—the way a younger, American author might have done (or at least been begged by her agent to do). Ferrante grants the lives of young girls—the jealousies of who walks next to whom, the subtle competitions and confidences—an operatic scope, trivializing nothing and putting interpersonal dynamics on par with international politics.

And at the center of everything is the Lenu/Lila bond. The bond is so central that it requires certain suspensions of

11. Whatever the fuck that term means? In industry-speak, it seems to primarily refer to work written by and about women and dealing with serious themes common in women's lives, but with less contradictory complexity of character and form and in more accessible prose than so-called "literary fiction." But in reality, that description wouldn't really hold. Had Eugenides's *The Marriage Plot* or Franzen's *Freedom* been written by women, it is highly likely they would have been categorized as "women's fiction." So let's just say that this term, which holds immense importance for the fate of a book in the actual publishing industry, is more or less a fabrication determined by the gender of the author and how many copies a marketing team thinks it can sell by putting "branded for women" type cover art on the book, releasing in paperback rather than hardcover, and aiming to get bulk orders from Costco and Target.

disbelief. For example, even prior to mid-life, despite Lenu's rich and varied life as a novelist, journalist and feminist critical theorist, as well as her proximity to intellectuals both literary and political and her multiple relationships with men, Lenu *never* seems to make another important female friend after going away to college in her teens. The key to buying in (unless we choose to label Lenu as somehow "unlikeable" and unable to make friends, which is not the conclusion I believe Ferrante means us to draw) lies in the fact that Lenu is "curating" her memoir as any memoir writer must: what does not concern the central theme of her relationship with Lila is not in the text, and only things that impact them *both* in some manner are delved into. Having written a memoir myself since reading the Neapolitan Novels for the first time, I feel more awakened to this knowledge in my most recent rereading of the quartet. After all, my own memoir—which focuses on divorce, infidelity, breast cancer, caregiving elderly parents, "getting out" of my old neighborhood, sexual awakening, guilt, the small boxes into which patriarchy tends to corral middle-aged women and mothers and the search for a way women can break out of those constraints without falling into self-destructive tropes—barely mentions Alyssa, despite her mammoth role in my life. When mentioned at all, Alyssa is not much "characterized," either, whereas my friendship with Angie—whom I stopped seeing regularly by my early twenties—is given significantly more depth. Angie, I reasoned, made a bigger impact on the aspects my memoir focused on, or at least so it seemed to me at the time. Or maybe it's this: if a real-life experiment were done that lifted either woman from the world entirely—a "George Bailey was never born" styled erasure—my *life* would be more radically changed, and for the extreme worse, by the absence of Alyssa... but perhaps my *psyche* would be more altered by the erasure of Angie, even though I rarely intersect with her anymore? It is hard to imagine who I might be, right now, had Angie and I not grown up together, or even whether I would be writing this book. Well, yes. By contrast, it is not unreasonable for me to wonder whether—without Alyssa—I would even still be *alive* right now, as she has been my grounding touchstone (after a more tumultuous early friendship) since I was around twenty-two. Of my many other close friendships in adulthood—my aforementioned writing group, for example, one of whom I have been tight with since we were in grad school in our mid-twenties—there is zero mention at all in my memoir unless you count the acknowledgments page. So it is my assumption that Lenu—the hypothetical "real person" of Lenu, the *author/narrator* of a memoir—is a woman who has a life that extends beyond the pages she is furiously typing, has friendships formed later in life and outside of her old neighborhood in Naples, but does not consider those friendships to have formed her deepest self, and so they are excised for a singular focus on Lila, to the extent that the role of Lila's other neighborhood friends supersedes, too, any friendships Lenu formed later on her own.

Lila and Lenu's friendship begins on a less than idyllic note, as did mine with Alyssa.[12] Lenu, fascinated by both Lila's intelligence and her physical and emotional toughness, begins to copy her—a theme that will echo throughout the

12. My friendship with Alyssa began when she confronted me in Catechism for having invited her best friend to my house to play, but never inviting her. She promptly announced that she was coming over after CCD, and we walked home together in the early stages of the now-infamous Blizzard of 1979, wading through snow drifts up to our waists, all of it infused with the heightened danger and surreality of childhood. Once at my home, given the terrible weather, Alyssa ended up spending the night—then school was canceled so she stayed longer. Though her apartment was only four or so blocks away, the snow was inhospitable and Alyssa's mother not the type to make heroic and extravagant efforts to come and fetch her child. Hence, she just remained. By the time we went back to fifth grade when school resumed, we were self-proclaimed best friends, setting off years of competition between Alyssa's now former best friend and myself as to who would "win" Alyssa—a more active and unpredictable love triangle, I will say having later been through some doozies, than I ever encountered when involved with a man.

series—following her around, until they find themselves playing with their respective dolls, Nu (Lila's) and Tina (Lenu's) near an open grate that leads to the cellar of local crime boss Don Achilles. When the two finally begin to engage in a more mutual play and swap dolls, Lila instantaneously and volitionally drops Tina, who is newer and better made than Nu, through the grates into the cellar. Whether she does this out of envy at the nicer doll, or because she is trying to provoke Lenu in some manner—to find out why this girl is following her and how far she will go with it—the reader does not know. (It is likely some combination of both.) Lenu shocks Lila by promptly throwing Nu in after Tina and saying, "[w]hat you do, I do." This prompts the two girls to descend into the terrifying basement, where it appears they are unable to find the dolls, become convinced that Don Achilles himself stole them and then steel themselves to go up to his apartment and demand their return. Seemingly amused by the concept that he would be stealing little girls' dolls, Don Achilles first mocks his young, gender nonconforming offspring Alfonso by asking if he took the dolls, then gives the girls a few coins, telling them to replace the dolls. Instead, the two girls buy the book *Little Women*, which changes the rest of their lives.

The incident with the dolls is extremely complex and

is never fully explained. At the end of the fourth book, *The Story of the Lost Child*, Lila's final act on the page is to send Lenu her old doll, Tina, in a crudely wrapped package with no identifying information, note, or return address. It is unclear what Lila means by this gesture, but it is rife with meaning considering that Lila's lost daughter, named Nunzia after Lila's mother, was nicknamed Tina, and the two women as adults have already discussed the coincidence. Is the return of the original Tina some kind of sign that Lila has found her daughter (unlikely?), that she is still alive (she could theoretically have arranged for a package to arrive after her death, given she is intelligent and crafty enough to have successfully orchestrated her complete disappearance), or is it a gesture of love and apology of some kind? Truly, it's impossible to pin down. For starters, the reader never uncovers how Lila came to be in possession of Tina to begin with, considering that the basement scene depicts the girls not finding the dolls.

Or does it? Lenu, less bold than Lila, initially stands back while Lila goes into the darkened corners sweeping around blindly for the dolls, and so—in Lenu's first person point of view—we are told that they come up empty. Did Lila, by contrast, actually find them? Did she hide Tina under her too-big shapeless dress somehow? Might she even have thrown

Tina into the cellar precisely *so* she could feign not finding her and then keep her for herself? Has she been holding on to Tina—the first thing of Lenu's that sparked her envy—all these years? There are other vague possibilities, but none seem to me to have teeth. Did Alfonso steal the dolls (my vote is no—how would he have even known they were there?); did Don Achilles's son Stefano, later Lila's husband, mysteriously return the dolls in some way years after the incident? If so, why would Lila not have told her friend immediately, as they would be long past the age of playing with dolls as a pastime? Rather it seems clear that from the get-go, Lila has exhibited some manner of manipulation and scheming that is beyond Lenu's ken—it never seems to occur to Lenu, even when she receives the package at the age of sixty-six, that Lila has had Tina the whole while or that the initial endeavor was a ruse to steal her doll. Without Lenu's having had this suspicion, it's hard for the reader to substantiate our own, and Ferrante never tells us what transpired. But if, as I did, the reader deduces in the end of the fourth book that Lila likely stole the doll nearly sixty years prior and kept the secret all these years, the ending reshapes, recolors, and recasts Lila throughout the novels, seeming to justify some of Lenu's later treacheries toward Lila even though Lenu was unaware of Lila's original betrayal.

While I would like to have a clear conclusion as to where Tina-the-doll came from, the disappearance of Tina and Nu is also a deeply successful component of the darkly magical world of Lenu and Lila's childhood, and one to which I can profoundly relate. Childhood, in my old neighborhood, was marked by basement "clubhouses" that were dark, strange-smelling, cold even in the summertime, and beyond the reach (read: interest) of adults. I had one in my own basement, where the kids on the block often congregated because my mother was the only one who provided some makeshift furniture like folding chairs and made instant lemonade for me to bring down and pass out in Dixie Cups. Even with this parental sanction, the clubhouse was a creepy place. At the age of twelve or thirteen, I would hear a same-aged friend boast in my clubhouse that her (over-eighteen) "boyfriend" would "fuck me even when I'm on the rag" because "he knows I'm clean." This is the last time I can remember using the clubhouse, as many of my peers were becoming involved with sex, drugs, older guys, and peripheral gang activities, and I was terrified of the violence and misogyny that permeated these activities and of the fact that I (chubby, bucktoothed, having not yet had my first period) would never fit in to the world my friends were entering even if I tried.

"I feel no nostalgia for our childhood, it was full of violence," Lenu says early in *My Brilliant Friend.* This is, of course, both a logical statement and completely untrue. Lenu is obsessed with her childhood. And I relate. For many years, it seemed to me that my childhood would be the defining marker of my life, the immovable force that shaped me, the place from which I had been exiled by my own choice in leaving, but which would prevent me from ever quite belonging anywhere else. I had not belonged *there* either, nor had my mother, who was not Italian or Catholic but a WASP who didn't marry until the age of twenty-nine or have her first and only child until she was nearly thirty-six; my father, at forty-six, was older than some of my friends' grandfathers.

To support her claims of her old neighborhood being unworthy of nostalgia, Lenu chronicles the constant violence, the proliferation of blood, the coarse manners, the not-uncommon occurrences of murder, all of which was true in the neighborhood of my youth as well. One of the first examples of which I was aware involved a close friend in first grade. She had a developmental disability that made her seem younger than she was, and I felt protective of her like an older sister. She often came to my house to play, chaperoned by her older brother, who was handsome and extremely kind to her. At school, I defended this girl frequently, fighting bullies on her behalf when other kids made fun of her and urged her to do things like pull down her pants. She soon transferred out of our (Catholic) school and was sent to a special residential school and diagnosed—almost assuredly incorrectly—with schizophrenia. Nobody in our neighborhood was ever *diagnosed* with anything unless it was an ulcer, a heart attack, or diabetes; mental health diagnoses did not generally exist in our world, and so this rumor served to "other" my friend even further. At some point prior to our teens, this friend was raped by a group of significantly older guys, and I heard through the grapevine that when her devoted brother attacked one of the men in an effort at revenge, he was sent to prison. My friend eventually disappeared from the neighborhood entirely.

But as Lenu indicates, this was not some rare or even particularly dramatic event. These things just *happened* in my neighborhood. Another classmate was gang-raped at fifteen by a group of adult men, and for good measure beaten with coat hangers and thrown down a flight of stairs; none of the rapists were ever seriously investigated much less convicted; assorted women in the neighborhood apparently provided them alibis; everyone claimed the victim was "a slut," to the extent that I remember my own mouth forming that word too, and the way it tasted like poison and woke me out of a kind of numb slumber I'd been in—and made me ever more determined to leave.[13]

And so on. A boy I'd gone to school with was shot and killed in the playground across the street from my apartment; my friend's younger sister, pregnant in her teens, was killed with her boyfriend when a rival gang came looking for his brother and, finding him instead, shot him through the window of his car, the bullet going through his body into his girlfriend's, killing them both and their unborn child, too. Yet another former classmate was literally bludgeoned to death by her downstairs neighbor, again at age fifteen, when she was attempting to stand up for her little brother. A young man who had not been "right in the head," according to the adults, shot himself some years after returning from Vietnam. My father's brothers dropped like flies—two in an

---

13. This particular incident has eerie echoes in in *My Brilliant Friend*, when the significantly older Solaras brothers take barely teenaged Ada Cappuccio, a fatherless daughter of the neighborhood's "mad widow," who lacks familial or economic status, out in their swanky new car together and clearly molest her for approximately an hour before returning her to the neighborhood. In what seems an effort to survive in an atmosphere that does not acknowledge rape (much less stat rape), Ada continues to keep the company of the Solaras brothers so as to reframe her fate as her own choice . . . and is predictably called a whore by both her male and female peers.

influenza epidemic as toddlers long before my birth, others in their fifties and sixties from alcoholism and heart disease, until by the time I was nine years old only my father and one other of the original seven were left standing. As late as 2004, one of my cousins, who had been shot once before, was shot again and killed in the old neighborhood. This, of course, does not even begin to cover the vendetta deaths of adult men embroiled in gang or Mob violence—stories to which I would not have been privy.

But nostalgia! I have it for the strangest of things. Alyssa's mother, who was divorced, as many of the younger women in the neighborhood were, worked full-time, and so Alyssa was already a latch-key kid when we became close in the late 1970s. She was tasked with the household cleaning, in ways entirely familiar to the characters populating the Neapolitan Novels, but rather foreign to most contemporary American teens. For Alyssa, each day was dedicated to a different task: laundry, dusting and vacuuming, changing the sheets and so on. As Lenu often accompanied Lila to her family's shoe repair shop, so I went to Alyssa's home nearly every day after school, assisting with chores that were challenging enough for two, not to mention just one, ten-year-old girl.

Alyssa's apartment, through no fault of her cleaning labors or her mother's (somewhat over the top) levels of hygiene, was infested with roaches from other apartments in the building; they scattered when you turned on a bathroom light, less bold than those in some of my other friends' homes, where they crawled right by your face if you tried to wash your hair in the sink, or ran over your sleeping bag the moment the lights were out. There was rarely anything to eat at Alyssa's, and what little was in the refrigerator was off-limits to us without her mother's permission, which was often not granted.

At the time, both my parents and I had a long list of judgments about Alyssa's mother, who went out frequently on the weekends, leaving Alyssa alone or with an aunt. Sometimes she brought men home, Alyssa hearing them through her bedroom wall or running into them on her way to the bathroom. I did not tell my parents this part, but an older cousin of mine bartended at one of the only local bars and he knew it all. My parents took this information to mean that Alyssa *needed* us and included her in everything, even little family vacations. But they were not—no one was, then, there—the type to challenge why such things would make us all judge a woman as we never would have a man, or to point out the radical double standard.

My view is different now. Alyssa's mother had thrown her abusive, heroin-addicted, car-thief husband out of the house, told him never to come back, and raised her daughter completely on her own. The number of women in our neighborhood—in this *world*—who cannot evict or escape an abuser is too long, across all social classes, to even attempt to chronicle, and often with sound reasoning such as fear for their lives or their families' lives. But Alyssa's mother had done it. She was a survivor who did whatever was necessary to take care of her daughter, and indeed her daughter turned out to have a sense of obligation—of, I dare say, nostalgia—to the environment of our youth and returned like some girl-power *Welcome Back, Kotter* to our underprivileged school and made a life of teaching there for nearly thirty-five years, suffering both through the neighborhood's gentrification *and* its pockets that held out and were passed over by gentrification entirely.

In my two-parent household, where my father was on disability by the time I was ten and my mother did not return to the workforce until I was fifteen, nobody made me wash the family laundry or change the sheets on my parents' beds; in my home, we could eat anything we liked, and if we weren't eating my father might follow us around the house with a fork full of pasta saying, "Eat, it's good," until you had to either snap at him or comply. I did not understand this as privilege when I was growing up—"privilege" was for the characters on TV, who had big houses like on *Happy Days* or a housekeeper like on *The Brady Bunch*. It did not include us.

Except that yes, of course it did.

Alyssa did laundry in a dank basement at the age of ten, whereas I sat around reading library books and starting my first "novel," or got driven to the suburbs to look at the fancy houses with my parents, who liked to drive around in the dark, when it was easy to see inside the brightly lit homes, to check out if the rich people had beams on their ceilings. My father was obsessed with ceiling beams.[14]

Yet one of the greatest sites of my childhood nostalgia was the underground cement foyer adjacent to Alyssa's basement. It had its own door—I suppose it was a storage unit of sorts, though nobody ever stored anything there. The door did not have a lock, as there was nothing inside to steal. It was here that Alyssa and I engaged in imaginary rituals and kept our most precious possession: a box containing "magical" objects like dried rose petals, a half-burnt candle and what may have been a guitar pick of mother-of-pearl, though we were not sure what it was when we found it.

---

14. In fact, one of my father's favorite ceiling beam destinations was the Deer Path Inn, in Lake Forest, IL, quite near the Ragdale Foundation, where I am writing this book, and where I just dined at the Deer Path Inn with Alyssa, who drove up to visit me for the occasion and toast my parents.

In this space, we obsessively read *The Changeling* by Zilpha Keatley Snyder, much as Lenu and Lila read *Little Women*, and our sacred objects were based on parallel objects in that novel, which was about a bold, curly-haired girl like me and a more reserved, good girl like Alyssa, though if I recall correctly, we were both too tactful (unlike Lenu and Lila) to ever explicitly identify ourselves with either character, as it was understood by us both that Ivy, with her wild curls, pointed face, talent for ballet and belief that she was a changeling, was the more compelling of the two, even if the other girl, Martha, would grow up to be a beautiful blond with money.

Alyssa and I cemented ourselves in this room—as Lenu and Lila did with *Little Women*—as "different" from the other girls.[15] While the other girls in the neighborhood

---

15. *My Brilliant Friend* closely reminds me, actually, of novels I had cherished in my childhood where friendship between young girls were central. And like Lenu and Lila, Alyssa and I, fantasized about writing a novel together based on our shared love of reading . . . we even went so far as to both write sections of a novel (we were about thirteen) and would at times pretend we were the characters from our story and act out various things we wanted to write later. But—like Lila—I also wrote in secret. Alyssa did not know that, from the age of ten, I had been writing on the cheap butcher block paper my mother bought me a series of novels about characters we had devised together, Genevieve (her) and Karen (me), who were orphans and led brutal and terrifying lives we used as an outlet for our fears and anger around violence we saw

aimlessly hung out on the corner or at the Shelter Court in the playground, waiting for some guy to claim them, we were full of ambition: begging our mothers for ballet lessons (I could write an entire essay on the comedically cheap school to which they finally relented to send us) and conspiring to write books or be famous actresses. I would go so far as to say that I felt magical in that mildew-smelling, cold, doored-off cement cell, and that I would have gladly spent hours there every day had Alyssa not been required to leave in order to go vacuum and dust and clean the dishes.

By the fifth grade, I had left Catholic school as my father, now on disability instead of tending bar, could no longer afford it, and was sent to the seemingly giant public school

---

playing out around us. Alyssa and I never finished (or got very far at all, actually) in our joint literary project, but by the time I had a driver's license I had written four Genevieve and Karen "novels," such as they were. While I hardly think anyone would ever read them and find evidence of some manner of genius, as Lenu does when she reads Lila's privately penned "The Blue Fairy," the novels served as a catharsis and holding place for me that allowed me to . . . well, at times to keep myself alive, and at other times to nurse my dream of getting out with—similarly to Lenu and Lila—unrealistic fantasies that if I could only publish a book, I would somehow be catapulted into another universe where I would have power, agency, and financial security. (Spoiler: Not so much with either the power or financial security part, but there remains no greater gift than the agency of being able to do what I love in life long past girlhood and to form an adult life in which my passions remain central.)

across the street, which both Angie and Alyssa had attended since kindergarten. Although Angie and Alyssa did not have an independent friendship without me, they got on fine—both were and are incredibly *kind* people—but Angie's devoted gang of girls greeted my arrival at their school with suspicion, jealousy and open hostility, while Alyssa's best friend (let's call her Maria) engaged in the kind of emotional warfare familiar to most twelve-year-old girls in an attempt to steal Alyssa back and ostracize me.

Those years were agonizing, as Angie, always the most beautiful and sought after, became involved with girls my mother called "fast," girls who made fun of me for being overweight, for never having made out with a boy, for using "ten-dollar-words." Alyssa, too, got a boyfriend (the only Black boy in our class and, if I remember correctly, the school), and she and Maria would traipse around talking about what they had done or not done with their boyfriends (Alyssa and hers decided on the sly to tell everyone they had made out because both were too shy to actually do it, but had they admitted such a thing our peers would have harassed them until they all but copulated in the playground for an audience). In the words of Lenu—or rather of the magnificent Anne Goldstein translations—"I suffered." I spent weekends weeping while Angie, who had been joined at my hip since we were three, disappeared to "parties" at which single moms got high with their daughters' friends and adult men were in attendance, and Alyssa and Maria pretended to sleep at each other's house while they really slept at Alyssa's boyfriend's house with two other boys in our class present, passing each other notes beforehand in school that said: *Don't invite Gina, she won't be any fun.* When I found the note, I wept in an open, hysterical way that frightened my parents. *I suffered*, yes, no tongue-in-cheek about it. Sunlight, kids happily playing ball, people going about their daily lives felt like an affront to me. I do not recall wishing terrible fates to befall Maria so that she might be removed as a threat, but if in fact I did it would not surprise me.

And, of course, I was also afraid they were right about me. Sure, I wanted to "be fun" and I wanted guys to like me, but I also had an idea of what life was *supposed* to be like that I'd gotten from novels, which I read voraciously, and the films my parents watched, and few reflected my own world back at me. If I, too, got a boyfriend, smoked pot before school, cut class, partied with adults, would I ever get out of this place or would I sink into a hole from which it was impossible to extricate myself?

Lenu faces similar dilemmas. While she enters middle

school, Lila is not permitted by her father—who cannot afford it and who also disdains the idea that she should be "educated"—to take the exam. Instead, she begins to work with her father and brother as shoemakers. No doubt out of envy and fears of inferiority, Lila also begins to align herself with other friends not going on to middle school either, predominantly Carmela Peluso, the daughter of the carpenter who went to prison for murdering neighborhood kingpin Don Achilles (though the reader is led to suspect Peluso is not guilty). Lenu immediately becomes a third wheel, writing, "When we went for a walk between the church and the stradone, Lila was always in the middle and the two of us on the sides. If I noticed that she tended to be closer to Carmela I suffered and wanted to go home." Yet, as it was for me, this hellish period, in which Lenu is afflicted with acne and prematurely large breasts, things soon shift: Lenu begins to succeed in high school, to learn more difficult subjects, she and Lila passing the baton of insecurity and pursuit back and forth throughout the novel, Lenu noting of Lila that "When she talked to me about Dido or her method for learning English words or the third declension or what she pondered when she talked to Pasquale, I saw with increasing clarity that it made her feel somewhat uneasy, as if it were ultimately she who felt the need to continuously prove that she could talk to me as an equal."

Whereas by the end of high school, Alyssa and I had grown out of our early jealousies and competition and began a more harmonious and adult version of best friendship that has remained with us for decades, Angie, by contrast, slipped ever further out of my grasp. She did not place into the selective-enrollment college prep high school Alyssa and I attended, and we began to lose track of her life. Increasingly, we no longer spoke the same language—not in the sense of dialect vs. Italian as with Lila and Lenu, but simply in our lifestyles, our friendships, our fashion, the types of music we listened to. Once, I ran into Angie at a mainstream dance club (I was more into "alternative music" by then and didn't normally frequent this club), and we did coke together in the bathroom: my first time, whereas by then she was dating an older guy who was intimidatingly handsome and had a dangerous reputation. We had not come to the club together but were unguardedly overjoyed to see one another. I did not have a "bad experience" from the coke; nothing harrowing happened; I remember the night as one of frenetic dancing, confidence, fun. Still, it was the last time Angie and I intersected in a social sphere of young people. Our lives diverged and we were swept up in separate tides.

I still loved her profoundly. As late as my early twenties,

when I was living with my ex-husband out east, I sometimes woke in the night crying after dreaming about Angie. I felt a kind of survivor's guilt: for my bachelor's degree, my quaint college town setting, my clean-cut Richie Cunningham boyfriend, my impending start of graduate school. I felt responsible for "abandoning" Angie to the neighborhood. She haunted me, and even though I was falling in love, was soon to become engaged, and was still incredibly close to Alyssa, I might well have cited Angie as the person I loved most, then, after my mother.

In other words, nostalgia gripped me. I never wondered if Angie *wanted* to be "saved"—if she had the slightest interest in college; if she would have dated my upwardly mobile but nerdy STEM genius of a boyfriend had he begged her to. I made assumptions about what she wanted or "should" want, then tortured myself with guilt about it, while meanwhile she was living her own life and would soon forge a path out of the neighborhood, too. I fancied myself more central to her ascent than I ever actually was, perhaps because I longed for her to need me the way I had once needed her protection in a place where she was in perpetual demand and widely admired, and I was the chubby daughter of a WASP who tended to hide in dark rooms with migraines. I felt guilty for my former envy of Angie, especially as I had come into a feminist consciousness and now categorized her father as having been "abusive;" I blamed myself for wanting to be like her—for wanting to *be* her—when in reality I'd had the easier youth. It's hard to say what she, in turn, felt about me. On the increasingly infrequent occasions on which we saw one another, she was always friendly and loving. Did she think of me when I was not around? Did she have any idea how central she still was in my consciousness?

While Alyssa and I eventually transcended competitiveness and envy, and the radically different paths Angie and I took recast much of what I had once believed true about our relationship, neither of these "plots" would make for a satisfying four-volume novel. Hence, Lenu and Lila's lifelong envy of the other, rather than driving them apart, binds them forever, even when it may seem a bit inexplicable to some readers. They each repeatedly forgive the unforgivable in one another; they each refuse to consider that the malice with which they not infrequently treat the other might be a sign that it is time to let go—and on the rare occasions distance is attempted, Lenu is haunted by Lila, as I was by Angie, and so she keeps returning, however far she roams. Nor does Lila let her go easily. As Lenu ages and would by all contemporary logic turn to newer friends with whom she might have more common interests, Lila remains a mythic figure to her: unparalleled, impossible to equal.

All this may seem hard to understand to younger readers weaned on a language of "boundaries" and "frenemies" and "toxic relationships," and in response to that implicit critique (*Why don't they just stop being friends already if they drive each other so crazy?*) many critics and savvy readers urge that you cannot understand the relationship between these women if you do not understand the nature of Naples in that era. I am sure they're correct (though I do not particularly understand the nature of Naples in that era, beyond what I have read in fiction). Even as an Italian American woman raised in such a similar (US-based) environment, with friendships that bore strong parallels to Lenu's and Lila's, I found myself more stunned than I remembered being the first time around by the ferocity of the women's frequent antipathy toward one another. As I began drafting this book, I even posted to Facebook in the summer of 2023 to see what other Ferrante fans thought about this, writing the following:

> Crowdsourcing question on female friendship! Bear with the backstory!
>
> So as many of you know, I'm writing about

Ferrante's Neapolitan Novels for Ig Publishing's "Bookmarked" series. In these novels, the character Lila is often randomly cruel to the narrator Lenu (they are lifelong best friends) out of envy and competition, as Lenu becomes more educated, cultured, and successful. This meanness is also juxtaposed with deep care, such as Lila buying Lenu's schoolbooks and making her promise many times to succeed academically. The push/pull between her fear of being outpaced vs. her genuine love for her friend and wanting her friend to succeed has always struck me as realistic, "normal," understandable, given what we readers understand of Lila's rather awful life.

Lenu, on the other hand, despite rising successfully for most of the 4 installments of the novel, baffles me a bit more. While it is absolutely true that Lila is portrayed relentlessly as gifted, exceptionally beautiful, and special, and seems to have the singular admiration of almost all who know her to the extent that it would be impossible to be close to her and not at times feel "second place" in everything, I am still finding aspects of Lenu's reactions to Lila to be . . . extreme . . . more so than

I noticed on first reading. From wishing Lila would miscarry her pregnancy to—numerous times—wishing Lila would flat out die, to also destroying Lila's journals/notebooks by throwing them in a river after she was the only one Lila entrusted them to, Lenu's envy of Lila . . . particularly as Lila's life is profoundly difficult . . . more and more strikes me as pathological, and not within the usual confines of even "frenemy" or competitive friendships.

I am curious what others think! I am not necessarily asking if you have ever wished your best friend would die or lose her baby or if you have destroyed the only personal private property she owned...or, hell, maybe I AM asking that? What I'm saying is that lifelong friendships are complex . . . and people, myself included, can be petty and envious . . . but does this particular behavior strike you as over the top, or genuinely par for the course in a friendship where there is a competitive dynamic? (Critics have definitely treated it as the latter.)

I think this struck me less powerfully the first time around because I was reading the books as they were released, spaced out, and isolated extremely negative thoughts seemed just "how some people are." Condensed this way, I found myself having a different reaction. I still LOVE the books! But Lenu is usually seen as the "good girl" and Lila as more malicious, and this read it struck me rather as the opposite, to a pretty intense degree.

I would love thoughts!

And thoughts I received! Some responses candidly revealed similar levels of love/hate in their relationships with friends (and sisters), while some writers whose tastes I usually feel aligned with like Joanna Rakoff, Marie Mutsuki Mockett, and Jennifer Banash—among others—indicated that this was the precise reason they had ultimately not been able to finish reading the series: that they felt (to collectively sum up a subset of women on my thread) Ferrante perpetuated the idea that female friendships are ultimately dominated by competition and malice, and that they could not imagine feeling anything of this sort toward their women friends and would not want to be friends with anyone who felt such things (That they should miscarry! That they should die! Who would destroy their journals when those writings were the one private outlet in the entire life of a woman denied education or bodily autonomy!), and that it seemed "pathological."

Many of the Facebook comments led to private Message threads, pointing me to sources on Ferrante or telling me long and involved personal stories of parallel relationships. The entire endeavor was, I must say, the most rewarding social media experience I've had in several years and reminded me how fortunate I am to have my own large cast of Brilliant Friends, and why I don't leave Facebook despite it essentially being the epitome of late-stage-capitalist bullshit.

But still, let's suppose for a moment that perhaps I was asking the wrong question altogether . . .

I have never in my life wished ill (honestly, of *any* kind that I can recall) on a female friend, even when I struggled with jealousy. But if I had flipped this question around and asked the entire population of my private Facebook page if they had ever felt these ways about a lover or spouse who jilted them . . . well, the specific details, the miscarrying and so forth, might be quite different, but I have a strong suspicion that far more people would have admitted ascent and understanding—and perhaps compassion for Lenu, even, in her wicked thoughts—than if we frame the relationship between the two women as "just" a platonic friendship. Aside from my own rather melodramatic divorce, in which I think it is fair to say that both my ex and I revealed an ugliness I had absolutely no idea either of us even *possessed*, there is also the truth that if I had $100 for every woman friend I've had over the course of my life who has hissed through her tears, "I wish he would just die!" after having her heart entirely crushed, I would be able to pay my taxes much more easily, or maybe even fund my youngest child's first semester at college. Do these friends *truly* wish death on men who have hurt them romantically? Well, of course not in a way that is lasting: ask them a few months, much less a few years, later, and most likely they feel either an utter indifference or even wish their ex well. But in the moment? If even half of them can be taken at face value, there are a whole lot of people going around wishing ill on one another in the heat of the moment.[16]

Needless to say, there were more than a couple of people on my Facebook thread who pointed out to me that Lenu and Lila's bond is as intense as a romance, and that (especially when they are adults and the usual rivalry of early teen friendships between girls has passed) looking at it *without*

16. Such heat of the moment thinking among men, of course, often leads to far more than vocalized wishes of harm in confidence to one's friends, and can translate into the phenomenon of intimate partner violence and murder, as it is a fairly open cliché that if a woman turns up dead, her male romantic partner or ex-partner is the immediate first person of interest, and statistically most likely to have killed her.

considering that lens is not actually . . . looking at it at all. As Ferrante herself says in a column she wrote for the *Guardian*, "The Italian word for 'friendship,' *amicizia*, has the same root as the verb 'to love', *amare*, and a relationship between friends has the richness, the complexity, the contradictions, the inconsistencies of love."

I believe that to be accurate. But/and I also believe Lenu and Lila are "more than friends," more, even, than the lifelong surrogate sisters Alyssa and I turned out to be. Theirs is also a (doomed) love story, full of the ups and downs of thwarted eroticism and fierce physical jealousy, even if entirely unspoken until the words Lenu types after Lila's disappearance, that we, in turn, are reading: her authentic confession. And for many contemporary readers, the question might be, *If this is her authentic confession then why doesn't she just go ahead and admit to being in love with Lila?* To which I might have a few answers, ranging from there barely existing a language for homoerotic desire between women in 1940s Italy to—on the other end of the spectrum of my own argument—*Well, doesn't she?* If we're reading carefully, doesn't Lenu tell us of her thwarted passion in various ways over and over again? And doesn't Lila, in fact, even respond in kind?

This is at its most pronounced in the inaugural book, *My*

Brilliant Friend, and positioned most strongly near the end of the novel, in a place of prominence, in the space in which novelistic epiphanies are often had and truths revealed. But its seeds are planted even earlier. When Lila—in order to avoid the attentions of one of the crime-entrenched Solaras brothers, both of whom are obsessed with her but the older of whom, Marcello, considers her his fiancée despite her never having consented to the role—becomes engaged to Stefano Carracci, son of the murdered crime boss Don Achilles, she and Lenu have the following exchange:

> "Do you love Stefano?"
>
> She said seriously, "Very much."
>
> "More than your parents, more than Rino?"
>
> "More than everyone, but not more than you."

I might even say that the relationship between Lenu and Lila is encapsulated in this encounter. The moment Lila has made this grand declaration, Lenu asks if she is making fun of her . . . but the reader (and the older Lenu, writing the story?) knows this is not the case. In fact, Lila, despite a marriage, a passionate affair, a longtime domestic partnership and two children, as well as the devotion of seemingly almost the entire neighborhood (more on that later), never seems to love *anyone* half as much as—or find anyone as essential as—Lenu, until the birth of her daughter Tina in the fourth book. Despite Lenu seeing herself as the dependent one in the relationship, as the one constantly in second place, Lenu is the one constantly on the move and de-centralizing her friendship with Lila, at times volitionally not speaking to her (sometimes with good reason and other times driven by her own insecurities).

Lenu and Lila are both jealous creatures, as women with little autonomy and a history of gendered oppression and trauma are encouraged to be toward one another. After all, if you have very little, and what little you have you did not necessarily choose, it is easy for envy to take root. Throughout the novels, Lila desperately wishes to have had the chance to study like Lenu—her passion for learning indicates not just an intrinsic academic genius but the sort of joy in scholarship that Lenu, who is given the opportunity to study and excels, does not possess. Lila therefore must entrust to Lenu the task of living *for her*, so that Lila may vicariously have the life she yearned for. The psychological burden of this is heavy for both young women. For Lila, Lenu is her only hope for a kind of secondhand contact with the wider world and someone with whom to discuss Latin,

English, literature. At times, she withholds such discussion, seemingly ashamed of her desire to devour books and learn languages, given that she has no more than an elementary school education, has been rejected and disparaged by the old teacher who once found her brilliant and has no hope of entry into Lenu's world. Yet she always returns, in some way, to trying to share her hunger for knowledge with Lenu—if she succumbs to her jealousy and excises Lenu from her life, she will have no further connection to that world, no matter how economically secure she may become. As such, it's not that difficult to fathom why Lila remains (albeit often passive-aggressively and sometimes just plain aggressively) devoted to Lenu. While man after man drops at her feet, and everything she touches—from a shoe store to a computer start up—seems to turn to gold from Lenu's perspective, Lila's life grants her zero proximity to the hallowed halls of higher learning. That Lila, when on rare chances she does meet intellectuals, dislikes them and finds them ridiculous, does nothing to quell her thrashing regret that she was not given the opportunity to pursue an education, or her hunger to obsessively learn.

Lenu's motivations may seem harder to fathom. While Lila alternates between wishing (and even demanding) the best from Lenu and then being cruel to her out of envy when

Lenu finds success, Lenu by contrast never seems—quite—to wish Lila well unless she herself can be thrust in the middle of it and made to feel essential to the outcome. When Lila is on the brink of marriage—to a man both she and Lenu, at that time, believe to be an ethical person and a good catch—Lenu candidly admits to the reader, "Inside it was what I truly wanted: to bring her back to pale, ponytailed Lila, with the narrowed eyes of a bird of prey, in her tattered dress. No more of those airs, that acting like the Jacqueline Kennedy of the neighborhood." This revelation feels both slightly startling (Lila, impoverished, seemed to own one dress and spent her childhood being beaten by her father and even her beloved elder brother), yet full of the naked candor that makes readers *trust* Ferrante, who does not stay on the clichéd path of "likable" and "sympathetic" heroines and allows characters to be petty, even fully shitty. The reader may wonder what continues to bind Lenu to Lila in that moment, as—nearing the end of *My Brilliant Friend*—having such a thought about one's alleged best friend might be enough to shame many of us into keeping our distance.

But Ferrante—in the only blatantly homoerotic scene across all four volumes—soon gives us a guidepost for Lenu's secretly cruel thoughts, as Lenu bathes Lila on her wedding day. The novels, this scene tells us, are not to be read precisely as the saga of a platonic friendship, however intense, or even the story of surrogate sisters: Lenu is, fairly blatantly, in erotic rapture at Lila—is in love with her, and Lila may (though we are not quite sure) be aware of this fact and may reciprocate it without ever entertaining any notion that it will *result* in anything. Goading Lenu by saying she will be late to her own wedding, Lila convinces Lenu to help her bathe. Clearly, it is highly unlikely this saved Lila any time . . . but it leads to one of the most revealing scenes of the novels. Lenu recalls:

> Today I can say that it was the embarrassment of gazing with pleasure at her body, of being the not impartial witness of her sixteen-year-old's beauty a few hours before Stefano touched her, penetrated her, disfigured her, perhaps, by making her pregnant. At the time it was just a tumultuous sensation of necessary awkwardness, a state in which you cannot avert the gaze or take away the hand without recognizing your own turmoil, without, by that retreat, declaring it, hence without coming into conflict with the undisturbed innocence of the one who is the cause of the turmoil, without expressing by that rejection the violent emotion

> that overwhelms you, so that it forces you to stay, to rest your gaze on the childish shoulders, on the breasts and stiffly cold nipples, on the narrow hips and the tense buttocks, on the black sex, on the long legs, on the tender knees, on the curved ankles, on the elegant feet; and to act as if it's nothing when instead everything is there, present, in the poor dim room amid the worn furniture, on the uneven, water-stained floor, and your heart is agitated, your veins inflamed.

Lest the reader want to object that this is not a queering of the narrative, to argue that awe is a predictable response to seeing the magnificently beautiful body of another young woman in a culture where modesty reigns and friends, mothers, daughters, sisters, seem to avoid seeing one another undressed in even the tiniest of apartments, Lenu's passion grows ever more inflamed:

> I had a confusion of feelings and thoughts: embrace her, weep with her, kiss her, pull her hair, laugh, pretend to sexual experience and instruct her in a learned voice, distancing her with words just at the moment of greatest closeness. But in the end there

> was only the hostile thought that I was washing her, from her hair to the soles of her feet, early in the morning, just so that Stefano could sully her in the course of the night.

Lenu concludes that "the only remedy against the pain I was feeling, that I would feel, was to find a corner secluded enough so that Antonio could do to me, at the same time, the exact same thing." What we are witnessing in this scene is not the "envy" we are quite accustomed to seeing in Lila and Lenu's friendship, but (*to pull her hair!*) an unspoken, primal, and intense sexual attraction that neither girl would have half the language to articulate even were their feelings utterly mutual and they shared a desire to transgress. Lesbianism and bisexuality are not part of the consciousness of the Neapolitan Novels, though they are surely recognized by Ferrante, an author writing in this century, in this scene. Lenu—who achieves sexual desire, ecstasy, and obsession with male partners, in particular her youthful boyfriend Antonio and her later longtime lover, Nino, with whom she has a child, seems to be clearly a bisexual woman, whether or not her attractions to women are limited to Lila. For her part, Lila does not seem to experience sexual desires, whether due to PTSD over so many severe beatings, or whether they are cut off by violent marital rape on her honeymoon that continues throughout her marriage to Stefano. Yet some thirty pages prior, we have seen her declare that she loves Lenu more than her soon-to-be-husband, more than her parents, more than her brother, more than *anyone*, and she is the one who initiates the bathing scene. Whether or not she is capable of reciprocating physical attraction, it seems clear that it was emotionally imperative to her to try to draw such a response out of Lenu.

It is on this note (the final scene of the book is Lila's wedding) that we leave our first installment. Ferrante's interesting choice to never give us another comparable scene—not to allow the eroticism to outweigh the psychology of lifelong friendship; not to turn this into either an explicitly queer love story *or* a story of Lenu's tragic desire for a woman who, due to PTSD or asexuality, cannot reciprocate—is, in my view, a wise one. Romantic and sexual love—as we will see—are not things to be trusted in the Neapolitan Novels, and are, without exception, either unrequited or fleeting, whereas Lenu and Lila remain bonded even after Lila's disappearance. In the operatic scope of turning girlhood into something mythic, we take in Lenu's love for Lila in the same way we take in her desire to see Lila entrenched in abject poverty again, or in the way we take her feelings of being incomplete when she does not have Lila off whom to bounce ideas and intellectual energy. The erotic love Lenu feels for Lila infuses physical descriptions throughout the four novels, but we will never see a moment of potential consummation again: doing so would relegate Lila to the domain of Lenu's other lovers (and Lila's) and—subversively—lessen their relationship's primacy and importance. Lenu and Lila are incomplete without the other, a truth that—for all it may feel so at the time—is true of none of their actual romantic/sexual relationships. They are, for one another, singular.

TWO

Beloved Character Syndrome: The Hyperrealism of Lila Cerullo

When I was getting my master's degree at the University of Illinois's Program for Writers back in the late 1990s, it was still perfectly acceptable—and taken by some as their absolute duty—to be rude and imperious to one's workshop peers. We had one memorable trio of women, for example, who would sometimes storm into the room, plop into chairs and burp loudly in tandem before telling a particular successful male writer in the program, who had been published in the *New Yorker*, that plot and character were dead and how infinitely boring and predictable he was. In this vein, a complaint I remember being lodged against one of my submissions of my debut novel, *My Sister's Continent* (later published in 2005), was that one of the two protagonists, Kendra, suffered from, in the words of our intelligent, incisive, and quite blunt professor, "beloved character syndrome." I do not know whether our professor made this term up—this was decades before "main character syndrome" would become common internet vernacular among Gen Z—but it was one of the most useful terms I've ever heard and learned of as a writer or an editor.

Essentially—again, years prior to the publication of the Neapolitan Novels—I, too, was writing a novel in which one of the two leads had gone mysteriously missing, and the other, her twin sister left behind, was attempting to tell the story of their family, based on memory and her sister's journals. The novel's narrator is an attractive, razor-sharp young woman who suffers from a variety of trauma induced maladies and host of insecurities, while her missing sister (Kendra) was always the bold one, the one who seemed confident in every setting, the one at whose feet men dropped even if she was disdainful of their attentions (and even if—as with Ferrante's Lila—these would-be-suitors did not treat her especially well once they attained her), the one whose beauty others always noticed immediately even though the two women essentially shared the same face.

As with Ferrante's Lenu, my narrator was portraying her missing twin sister *as she had seen her*, through a worshipful, intimidated, envious lens. Fair enough: this formula is not particularly unusual. From *The Great Gatsby* to *The Last of Her Kind* by Sigrid Nunez to *The Invisible Circus* by Jennifer

Egan to *The Interestings* by Meg Wolitzer to *The Mysteries of Pittsburgh* by Michael Chabon to *The Secret History* by Donna Tartt, it is not uncommon for a novel's narrator or main character to be/fall under the thrall of a more overtly charismatic character (or characters) of whom they have an inflated opinion based on their estimation of themselves as comparatively ordinary or less glamorous, mysterious, or magnetic. The problem, however, as my professor pointed out, was not that my *narrator* might find her twin sister to be so extraordinary and special, it was that essentially every single character in the novel not only reinforced this same view, but that a plethora of scenes seemed to exist just so that the other characters could talk about and analyze this "beloved" character, further spotlighting her, and that although there might be sketches and outlines standing in for what other characters' lives were like when the Beloved Character was not present, on the whole it appeared as though the novel's cast of characters all seemed to revolve around the Beloved Character, existing merely to be obsessed with her, no matter how much time may have passed and no matter what else they might have going on in their lives. In other words, when the Beloved Character is not on the page, all the other characters ever do is think about her. She dominates their inner lives. They do not quite appear to have lives of their own, even if they are engaged, have jobs, go to therapy, have parents and children, make mistakes. Everything is held in relief to the Beloved Character, who motivates the actions and dominates the psyche of every character in the book.

Reader, I revised.

Charismatic-but-troubled people make excellent protagonists, and sometimes do suck rather a lot of emotional and intellectual energy from those in their sphere. However, I did get what my professor meant, and my own relationship with Angie—though neither character in my debut novel is based on her—helped me to grasp it.

At this point, I was in my late twenties. I was living in Chicago again with my first husband, and I'd entertained fantasies that this would spark a new adult bond between Angie and myself, and that we would somehow recapture that childhood closeness. But although we continued to see each other at weddings and funerals and the occasional graduation party of people in our old neighborhood, and we always hugged and gushed extravagantly of our desire to see each other again soon, for the most part that rarely happened, and my life in Chicago as a married woman in graduate school went on without her—as her life in Chicago had been going on without me for some time.

—

Alyssa and I remained very close—she even lived in our ground floor apartment for a while when she finally left her mother's house—but that single relationship did not dominate my life either. I made friends in grad school, and for a time they seemed the center of my life almost more than my own husband. My grad school friends and I did everything together: sat in three-hour seminars (during which we sometimes wrote notes back and forth to one another like junior high kids), witnessed departmental scandals and gossiped endlessly about them, were in a writing group every Friday night, hung out at the bar where one of our members bartended, exchanged writing, discussed and shared books. We were together so much that we all seemed to even share the same fashion aesthetic, every woman's lips a shock of almost-black cherry, every dress vintage—oh the plethora of beaded and embroidered old cardigans! In any case, none of these people are "important" to this book, even though they were deeply important to *me*. Rather, my point is that it is hard to replicate Beloved Character Syndrome in an actual lived life, which is precisely why it can seem problematic in fiction. Even Alyssa, who had once known Angie fairly well and semi-idolized her as we all did back then, had quite forgotten all about her in the midst of her own busy life of managing a first-grade classroom. Eventually, I introduced her to one of my classmates and the two rapidly fell in love and married, starting their own family.

Unlike in *Gatsby*, unlike in the Neapolitan novels, in real life, even if we do not suffer from so-called Main Character Syndrome, we are quite stuck being the protagonists of our own lives; the "peripheral narrator" is, excepting in cases of great dysfunction, a craft invention. Real-life collective groups of people don't generally go through life always and only thinking of *one specific other person* about whom they all mutually share an obsessive interest. While in some families, there may be one person who takes up all the air, even then once we leave our homes, nobody *else* considers our father/mother/brother/sister to be the mythic creature (as wonderful or as horrible) as we do, and if they do it is to commiserate, not because that menacing father or beautiful sister is at the center of their *own* existence, too.

What my professor was saying, then, was that even when someone's role in your novel is as a "supporting character," you must write them as though they are the main character of their own life, not as if the only purpose they ever serve is to talk about and further the plot surrounding your

Beloved Character. Further, said my professor, the more you succumb to Beloved Character syndrome in your work, the less the reader will *actually love* this character you're working overtime to sell them.

One of the most intoxicating and least realistic aspects of the Neapolitan Novels, then, is that Elena Ferrante either did not receive, or tore into a million pieces, the Beloved Character Syndrome memo. In the world of the Novels, Lila Cerullo is the center of almost everyone's emotional life. We know that this is true of Lenu, who even does such things as seeming to "channel" Lila when she's nervous, behaving brazenly as she imagines her friend would, such as showing her breasts to a group of boys for money instead of bolting in terror as she wants to.

But it does not stop there, as it most likely would in real life. Rather, Ferrante goes for broke. Lila begins receiving declarations of love by the age of fourteen, not, predominantly, from her same-age peers but from a host of men, some of whom are nearly a decade older. (The complexity of the issue of male vs. female ages in the Neapolitan Novels is a tangle in itself—almost none of the central boys/men in the novel are the same age or within a two-year difference of Lenu and Lila.) Setting aside for the moment that a man in his twenties taking a serious romantic interest in a girl of fourteen would now be considered stalking at best and stat rape if the two were to actually embark on a "relationship," and surrendering to the fact that we are both in another country and starkly different era where it was not unusual for girls to marry by about the age of sixteen (this was true in the generation immediately prior to mine in my old neighborhood, too, so it is not a stretch of my particular imagination—one of my cousins married at fourteen, with her parents' permission), logistical issues still abound.

For starters . . . where *are* all the girls who are the same age or just slightly younger than these men: Pasquale, Marcello and his brother Michele, Enzo, Nino, Stefano, and so on? They seem not to exist. When fourteen-year old Lila begins to receive proposals—first from Pasquale, who is in his early twenties, then from Marcello who is twenty, then finally from Stefano, who is eight years her senior—are we to assume that all the girls in an age-appropriate dating pool are long since married, and that fourteen-year-olds are all these men have to choose from? If that is the subtext, Ferrante never spells it out. It also fails to consider *how* three of the richest eligible bachelors in the neighborhood, Marcello, Michele, and Stefano, have managed to remain uncoupled when surely all the girls of their own age would have had designs on them.[17] But while a whole paper could surely be written about the age differentials between men and girls in the Neapolitan Novels, for our purposes here the fact remains that each one of these young men would have gone to elementary school with girls their own ages; each would be attractive to girls only slightly their junior if taking a younger wife was seen as culturally desirable, and yet it is as if none of these men have even *met* another woman outside of Lila and her gaggle of friends, and—to my point here—each falls in extreme and lasting love with Lila, such that the only man who ever seems to really "get over her" in his life is her ex-husband Stefano. Otherwise, men remain devoted to Lila unwaveringly.

Among these men are Pasquale, son of the carpenter convicted of killing Don Achilles—an ardent Communist, political and passionate; Stefano, the son of Don Achilles, who runs a successful grocery store that eventually spools into a chain of businesses, making him quite rich; and Michele and Marcello Solaras, whose mother is the neighborhood loan shark and who flashily show off their dirty money at every opportunity while being, Lenu tells us, extremely handsome. Then there is Enzo, a quiet boy

17. When these men do couple, notably it is with girls the same age or younger than Lila.

who sells fruit from a cart and falls in love with Lila in childhood, though he does not declare himself until she has left her first husband and is destitute, pregnant and alone. Both Antonio and Nino—two men with whom Lenu has relationships—also display an obsession with Lila. Antonio defies the orders of the Solaras brothers in order to protect her, even though he would be at best fired and at worst killed should he be found out, while Nino, who has an affair with Lila early in her marriage and briefly lives with her after she leaves her husband (before Antonio beats him up on the direction of the Solaras brothers) many years later, while involved with Lenu, who has his daughter, continues to beg Lila to sleep with him, to run off with him, claiming (though Nino is often full of shit, so who knows, really?) that he has been in love with her this entire time and was only with Lenu for the chance to be close to her. Michele Solaras, depicted as a heterosexual young man, is so singularly obsessed with Lila that he eventually embarks on a sexual affair with Alfonso, Lenu and Lila's queer, femme-expressing friend (the same child Don Achilles accused of stealing the girls' dolls), once Alfonso begins to emulate Lila, copy her style, and make himself[18] into as close a replica of

---

18. It would be my inclination to identify this character as a trans woman, as this is the life Alfonso seems to be living by the end

her as he can manage. When, in the second installment, *The Story of a New Name*, Lila is pregnant with another man's child, jobless, and in danger from both her husband and the Solaras brothers, Enzo—one of the only truly "good guys" in the entire series—steps forward to pledge himself to her, leaving his longtime girlfriend Carmela ("Carmen"). When Lila herself asks, "And Carmen?" Enzo answers simply, "You are much more important." He goes on to profess, "I've loved you since we were children. I never told you because you are very beautiful and very intelligent, and I am short, ugly, and worthless," before urging Lila to return to her husband but promising that if Stefano abuses her, he will kill him if need be and go away with Lila. Though he does not in fact kill Stefano, Enzo and Lila do eventually leave the neighborhood together, where Enzo lives chastely with her for some years without complaint before Lila finally decides to join him in his bed and the two have their daughter, Tina.

If it were only men who seemed to be centrally obsessed with Lila, even their disparate ages and the implied lack of any other beautiful, charismatic, or intelligent girls in their entire neighborhood notwithstanding, the reader might be

---

of the final book, but I will refer to Alfonso by a masculine pronoun given that this is how Lenu refers to him in the novels, set, of course, before gender identity was widely understood in contemporary terms.

able to buy in fully: after all, there are women (and men) who possess an extraordinary sexual energy and draw lovers and acolytes in droves, and if the sheer number of men devoted to Lila over the course of a lifetime seems a bit excessive, it is in general keeping with the amplified, dramatic nature of the books. But *everyone* seems focused on Lila—nobody fails to notice her even if they initially seem to have done so. The girls' elementary school teacher is so distraught that Lila's family refuses to send her on to further schooling that she shuns Lila for it with a hyperbolic malice, later admitting to her cousin of Lila that "in her entire career as a teacher she had never had such a good student." The girls' childhood girlfriends all copy Lila's mannerisms, opinions, even fall in love with the boys Lila suggests as a kind of experiment, to see if her power over them is as great as it seems. (It is, and Lila is distraught about it.) Lenu's parents, who initially disdain Lila and, in her teens, take to calling her a whore, end up seeing her as a kind of neighborhood savior; Lenu's mother in particular drives her envious daughter mad by relentlessly singing Lila's praises. Lenu's former beloved professor (who never taught Lila) ends up taking more of an interest in Lila than in Lenu; Lenu's own daughters, in the final book, love Lila madly and seem to prefer her to their mother, constantly going downstairs to her apartment when she and Lenu live in the same building after Lenu finally leaves Nino. And so on, such that if one made a map of characters (well, Ferrante actually does so at the opening of each book), one of the only characters in the entire saga who does not seem overly invested in Lila is Lenu's husband (then ex-husband) Pietro Airota, who originally dislikes her but comes around to friendliness that falls into the range of normalcy . . . but Pietro is also portrayed as, while generally a "nice" guy, incredibly self-involved and without much in the way of social skills and insight—or at least that is how Lenu sees him.

It is hard to know exactly what Ferrante's intentions were with this relentless illustration of Lila's "specialness." On the one hand, in a tight-knit neighborhood in a small town, there can be a kind of "group think," and if one important person takes a special interest in someone, it might fall to reason that others would follow. It would be fair to say that in my old neighborhood, there was widespread consensus that Angie was "special:" prettier, tougher, stronger, somehow more interesting than the rest of us. But this group think was fleeting—even in the closed system of our neighborhood, other concerns eventually occupied people, and by the time Angie was in her late teens, the collective consciousness of the neighborhood no longer seemed laser focused on her.

The collective Lila-worship exceeds that level (e.g. various men with whom Lila has never even been romantically involved gladly risking their lives for her and abandoning other women who love them in order to do so, and this kind of thing going on for *decades*). We could theorize, perhaps, that Lenu is so overcome with envy for Lila that she *interpreted* their lives this way but may not always have been correct . . . but many of these scenes are rooted in events, such as Enzo moving in with Lila though she will not sleep with him; Pasquale, Marcello, and Stefano all proposing; and Michele's obsession with Lila being the absolute center of his life and driving him to madness. It would be difficult for Lenu to distort all of this merely to suit her own agenda and worldview.

What is it, then, that Ferrante, Lenu, and the entire cast of the Neapolitan Novels believe is so singular about Lila? She is ferociously intelligent, teaching herself other languages while working in her father's shop and having no mentorship or schooling, taking out library books under the names of every member of her family and reading them all within the week. But having grown up in a similar environment that was, if anything, less provincial for having been a quarter century later, I feel pretty confident when I say that brilliance alone is not usually such an aphrodisiac to blue collar, machismo men. Although an argument can be made that Lila is the prettiest girl of her own age/grade level in the neighborhood, surely there are *some* other girls, even if not Lila's precise age, who also possess great beauty? Lila is stubborn, often rude, reckless and dangerous—when she is not even a teenager yet, she holds a knife on one of the Solaras brothers and threatens to slit his throat for grabbing Lenu's wrist. This kind of passion and intensity would surely get some men's blood boiling with lust, but others—male and female alike—would interpret this kind of behavior far less charitably, deducing that Lila is "crazy" which would cause them to avoid, dismiss or do her harm.

It defies the laws of reality for one girl to be so universally central and held on a pedestal in the lives of such a large cast of characters, and therefore, I find myself more and more leaning toward an embrace of Ferrante as a writer of hyperrealism, as O'Rourke notes in *The Guardian*, and of this being true across many of her novels, not only the Neapolitan Novels. While the term is more often associated with novels that contain blatantly "unreal" circumstances, such as William Gibson's *Neuromancer*, on the basic level hyperreality is simply the blending of what is "generally regarded as real" and "what is understood as fiction" seamlessly together so that there is no longer "any clear distinction between where one ends and the other begins."[19] While labels like "mythical" and "operatic" are often applied to Ferrante's work, mentions of hyperrealism are made only in passing, presumably because Ferrante's novels are lacking overtly "magical" or "sci-fi" elements. But whether the "author" of the text is meant to be one of its main characters, as with Lenu in the Neapolitan Novels, or whether Ferrante provides a less elaborate construct to how a book has come into existence, there is a hyperrealist element to *many* of her novels, where things veer just slightly over the top, just slightly within the realm of what might be seen—in the parlance of French feminism for example—as "hysterical writing," and one would have to be dozing off to interpret this as unintentional.

In the 2019 documentary *Ferrante Fever*, the Italian novelist Francesca Marciano speaks about the way Ferrante "digs" into her characters, and just when the reader is thinking essentially, *Okay, yes, I get it*, she digs some more, until the reader is forced to confront uncomfortable truths in their own psyche. Ferrante's use of hyperrealism is, I would argue, intended much as it is defined in the art world. In "A Matter of Term—Realism, Naturalism, Hyperrealism,

19. Tiffin, John: Terashima, Nobuyoshi (2005). "Paradigm for the third millennium," *Hyperreality*.

Surrealism," published on the website of the Academy of Fine Art Germany, hyperrealism is defined as follows:

> The goal of hyperrealistic art is often to create a kind of false reality. A "perfect copy" already requires a lot of artistic skill, but these artworks go even farther: They pose as a qualitative "improvement" of the original, in which shadows, light effects, surfaces and textures are depicted much more clearly than they are actually perceived in reality. This stirs different emotions in the viewer than the original.[viii]

The difference, then, between realism and hyperrealism is that "the former 'copies' a picture, while the latter consciously aims at creating specific feelings and emotions in the viewer."[ix] If this does not describe the worlds created by Ferrante—and here, specifically, by Lenu—I am not sure what it does describe. In the parlance of literary craft, we might say that Lenu's narrative in the Neapolitan novels aims to capture emotional truth more than fact, and if we look at Ferrante's earlier works, for example the cult classic, *Days of Abandonment*, we see that this is not a style "invented" strictly for Lenu, but the overarching ethos of Ferrante's writing in general. She is capturing emotions that are so real she amplifies them as *more real than real.*

We see this echoed in the almost picaresque style in which characters unlikely to have encountered each other in real life—or if they did, not more so than in passing—end up as central in each other's lives, as though the entire population of Naples, both intellectual and blue collar, consists of about fifty people Ferrante throws into various configurations of situations and relationships. Much as every single character in the novels worships Lila, so nearly every article written in a newspaper is penned by Nino's father, Donato Sarratore (who also molests Lenu at fifteen and later devirginizes her with her nominal consent when she is eighteen). Pasquale, much older and extremely poor, ends up the lover of Lenu's professor's highly educated daughter Nadia (who, incidentally, is even younger than Lenu and Lila) and goes on the run with her for political crimes in the fight against fascism; Nino pops up like a bad penny everywhere and is known by *everyone* wherever Lenu goes—in fact he, too, dates Nadia, as well as Lila and Lenu; Nino's sister, Marisa, despite having been out of the neighborhood since her early youth, ends up in a marriage of convenience to Alfonso and the lover of Lila's former husband Stefano; Lila, a young and impoverished mother working in a factory, ends up the darling of the Communist intellectuals who court her as somehow absolutely crucial to their missions. In other words, coincidences abound, and they do not attempt to justify themselves; we are just to take them as a given. They achieve the emotional impact for which Ferrante/Lenu is searching, and so, presto, they become real.

Were Ferrante writing the Novels in third person, these coincidences, the emotional hyperrealism, might strain credulity to the point of causing frustration, but because we are so deeply in Lenu's consciousness they create, rather, the desired impact of amplifying our emotions, of—as Marciano says—a digging that goes beyond our comfort level to reveal truths that may make us cringe. James Woods' now seminal piece on Ferrante in the *New Yorker* says as much, likening her descriptions of motherhood in *Days of Abandonment* to a world in which "children are seen as hideous enemies from a horror film" and saying "There is a foul brilliance in how Ferrante sticks with the logic of Olga's illogic, so that an ordinary enough complaint about the difficulty of raising children becomes an outsized revulsion, and the stink of motherhood leads inexorably to the incestuous end of all marital eros."[x] With Ferrante, exaggeration makes things more real rather than less. The magnification, the glorious "hysteria" of it all, forces us to see things in ourselves that most novelists would gloss over, and some readers might believe they would rather not look at too closely in themselves. Yet the sheer fact that Ferrante is an international phenomenon indicates that we *hunger*, rather, to look so deeply—that we are relieved, validated, achieve a kind of catharsis and recognition in the extremity of it all.

In making Lila such a Beloved Character, so unique in every possible setting, so beyond comparison with any other woman (or man), is Ferrante attempting to make us love her, as my old workshop professor complained, and laying it on too thick, ignoring the complex inner lives of other characters? Or, by contrast, is she attempting to throw us against our will into the tumult of Lenu's mind, in which no matter how far she goes or how high she rises, she will always carry the belief that, had Lila been beside her, Lila would have outshone her in every instance? Is she, even, with the allegiance we may unwittingly develop for Lenu as our first-person narrator, attempting to develop in the reader the same love-hate antipathy for Lila that Lenu possesses? Or, is she aiming for all of the above?

Ferrante has described romantic love as being beyond logic and reason, and female friendship as being "left without rules. Male rules haven't been imposed on it, and it's still a territory with fragile codes." To any familiar with Second Wave feminism, as Ferrante clearly is, this can't help but evoke the calls to action by Cixous, Irigaray, and others to invent a new language for women's writing, to write our bodies, to write outside the "Father's Tongue," and the embracing, in certain circles of feminist theory, of the figure of the hysteric as a kind of outlaw who exists outside the codes of the phallocratic order and will not conform. In this sense, whether we love her, hate her, or feel something conflicted and in-between, Lila—who Lenu says will not "be reduced," who will not conform even at the age of fourteen when she rejects Marcello Solaras's proposal—is more than just the friend of whom Lenu is envious, with whom she is obsessed, and whom she loves and hates at times in equal measure, but a kind of radical feminist outlaw, though Lila herself would likely mock the concept. And Lenu, ever her mirror, renders her with a hyperrealist prose that exists outside of "male rules" of language, of "realism," of order.

THREE

Class, Violence, and Gender

To say that so-called mobsters existed at the absolute top of the social hierarchy in my old neighborhood would, I believe, be entirely accurate. While I was in graduate school listening to one of my Italian American professors complaining about the patronizing reduction of Mafia stereotypes amid the height of *The Sopranos*' popularity, at the men's club in my neighborhood where my father went to (occasionally) shoot craps and (mainly) watch other men—many of whom were ex-cons—gamble, as well as to eat extravagantly homecooked meals comedically straight out of *Goodfellas*, the regulars were glued to "the Club's" TV on Sunday nights, watching Tony and his crew with great appreciation and reverence.

It's well-documented in my body of writing online that legendary crime boss Joe "The Clown" Lombardo lived across the street from my house when I was growing up, but the criminality to which I had access had nothing to do with any high-level Chicago outfit. My closest encounter with Lombardo had to do with his once buying all my M&Ms when our school forced us to go door-to-door peddling them and my father, ever cynical, told me, "Just go to Joe's house first," which confused me. But when I arrived, Joe said, "I'll take them all," and I ended up winning the ugly vinyl jacket we received as our dubious prize.

Other vague memories of our neighborhood's most infamous figure include Lombardo and his wife getting up and dancing to the theme song of *The Godfather* at my cousin's wedding, and everyone clearing the floor out of some combination of respect and the irreverent humor of our neighborhood so that Joe and his wife danced alone while everyone watched in admiration, no one to my knowledge snapping photos, as Lombardo was well known for holding a newspaper in front of his face (with eyes cut out) when the media attempted to take his picture.

When I was fourteen or so, Lombardo was sent to prison for bribery, and at our annual Fourth of July block party—during which an Italian flag was always painted on the pavement of our street—that year, the local news showed up and interviewed some of the neighborhood residents, inserting Lombardo into the conversation, which caused many of them to rhapsodize about how much they missed Joe coaching Little League (to my knowledge, there was no Little League) and being, in general, an impeccable neighbor and generous benefactor.

When he was released from prison in 1992, Lombardo did a kind of neighborhood lap by car, and stopped in front of our house honking loudly as a salute to my father, who—although only seven or eight years older than Lombardo—was by then a neighborhood patriarch of sorts, as the men in our neighborhood tended to die young, and by the time my father was in his sixties, he was among the last men standing of his own former peers. When my father apparently once asked Lombardo, whom he referred to as "a good kid," why he still lived in the old neighborhood even though he had "more money than God," Lombardo replied, "This is the only place in the world where I don't have to look over my shoulder."

All of which is to say that the culture of my neighborhood existed far from the lofty earnestness of Italian American academics who were wringing their hands at the reduction of our ilk to criminal stereotypes. Even among men like my father, who were not involved in organized crime, everyday transgressions were utterly normalized: we were forever feasting on filet mignon that had "fallen off the truck." At the aforementioned Fourth of July block party, the infinite supply of meat on the giant grill was said to come from a hole blown through the wall of a chicken factory.

Of course, there was a dark side to this. At school, we had no social workers or counselors (or, in fact, science books) and when a classmate showed up covered in bruises, everyone averted their eyes, and teachers asked no questions. If you heard a child screaming in fear or pain from inside an apartment—or for that matter saw someone casually beating their kid in public—you minded your own business.

Even when Alyssa was raped by one of our longtime neighborhood friends, it never occurred to her to report the crime or tell her mother. The rapist had an incarcerated father, like Alyssa's, and brothers who had been killed in gang violence, and Alyssa, even as she struggled with borderline agoraphobia in the aftermath of the rape, felt sorry for her assailant and the "damage" he had suffered amid so much intergenerational trauma.

I did not feel sorry for him. I was enraged; I wanted revenge. But even that, in our neighborhood, was a kind of quicksand. Nobody trusted the police, and justice and revenge were usually doled out through adult men with connections to those who could obtain it for you—but for that to happen, these men would have to share your worldview that an injustice against you had actually been committed. Being raped by a man whose home you had voluntarily entered (after drinking, no less), with whom you were hanging around, was not included among actionable offenses. Even my father, to whom Alyssa was like a second daughter, and who was widely known to be among the most progressive men in the neighborhood (he was certainly the only one I knew who voted for Mayor Harold Washington), scoffed when I called what had happened to Alyssa "rape." She had been sleeping at his house, my father "explained," which couldn't be done if you didn't want sex, because men were just "like that." Never mind that the rapist's mother also lived in the house and had known us since girlhood; never mind that Alyssa was fast asleep at the time the attack began and had not so much as kissed or held hands with her rapist, a platonic friend she thought of as a brother. Transgressions of this type did not "count."

To have *counted*, I realize now, Alyssa would have needed a father or brother against whom the rape was considered a sign of disrespect. But like the Neapolitan Novels' Ada Cappuccio, raped by the Solaras brothers without repercussion, Alyssa had neither. She had no man in her home to defend her honor—or rather, to defend his own. Girls and women did not, in our world, possess honor intrinsically:

it was a thing bestowed upon us vis-à-vis our association with men.

Like Lenu and Lila, I was obsessed with reading, and so I had a deep conviction that the culture of our neighborhood was not universal—that things were "different" elsewhere. My father often disagreed with this belief and thought it naïve; even though he had been born in the neighborhood (in my old bedroom, with a midwife) and had never lived anywhere else, he was utterly convinced that "there is no other place; every place is the same."

It turns out that we were both wrong and both right.

In places of poverty, where there is seemingly no "law" and where nobody is watching except those who possess no power, abuses can be flagrant, out in the open, utterly unashamed. As a girl, I believed this meant that among the middle-class, the educated, certainly the wealthy, these abuses did not *exist*, and conflated escaping from my neighborhood with escaping from the patriarchy and a culture of misogyny entirely . . . a notion of which I would soon be disabused, as is Lenu. Money can buy things, but it cannot buy male privilege. It also, Lenu concludes, cannot buy the elusive breeding, class, entitlement, and confidence she sees other girls exhibiting, both in the heart of Naples and embodied in the daughter of Professor Galiani, Nadia, who is dating Lenu's longtime crush, Nino. "She was superior to us, just as she was, unwittingly," Lenu tells the reader in *The Story of a New Name*, "And this was unendurable."

It is possible to attain money, to attain education, but Lenu—who did not even grow up brushing her teeth—is increasingly tormented by the notion that one can never outrun the past. This is perhaps most explicitly stated at the end of *My Brilliant Friend* when, despite the lavishness of Lila's wedding to Stefano, Lenu concludes:

> The plebs were us. The plebs were that fight for food and wine, that quarrel over who should be served first and better, that dirty floor on which the waiters clattered back and forth, those increasingly vulgar toasts. The plebs were my mother, who had drunk wine and now was leaning against my father's shoulder, while he, serious, laughed, his mouth gaping, at the sexual allusions of the metal dealer. They were all laughing, even Lila, with the expression of one who has a role and will play it to the utmost.

This fear dogs Lenu, despite her progressive politics and

sympathies with communist thought. She concludes that, "Merit was not enough, something else was required, and I didn't have it nor did I know how to learn it." We watch her like a slow-motion train crash as she attempts to marry into it, in absence of any convincing romantic love. Of her future father-in-law she says, "Professor Airota was an immortal god who had given his children magical weapons before the battle." She sees her boyfriend, Pietro, as "perfect in his overcultivated courtesy" and his sister, Mariarosa, as "invincible" due to having been born into culture, impeccable breeding. "I?" Lenu asks the reader, "I could only remain near them, shine in their radiance."

It is not only breeding and class that continue to mark Lenu's life, but also her fate at being a woman. As she continues her education, attending parties at professors' homes and marrying into the intellectual and affluent Airota family, men still hold court in classrooms, in literary journals, at parties, with their all-important opinions, while women sit by quietly listening. When she has children with the allegedly "perfect" Pietro, he barely lifts a finger to help her, shutting the door to his office so he can get his work done, never mind that she, too, is already a published author and has writing to do. Meanwhile, Lila, married to Stefano at the age of sixteen, is flush with cash, lives in a modern apartment at which Lenu gawks with awe, and can hand out money to whomever she wishes and dress like a film star just to walk down the stradone—but she is subject nightly to marital rape and beatings if she resists. Both women face lifelong (if unnamed) PTSD over their sexual assaults, neither of which take place in a context of impoverishment but are inflicted by men who have money in their pockets and whose lives are far from "hopeless" or unremitting despair. And both understand violence as commonplace, as part of what it means to interact with men, or—as Lila's mother casually says, "One day you're getting hit, the next kissed." It is a great strength of the Neapolitan Novels, and of Ferrante's treatment of gender in general, that she does not trivialize the constant misogyny to which women of every social class and age are subjected, even while she does not necessarily portray them all as equally life-threatening.

For it *would* be facile to attempt to equate the brands of gender-based discrimination Lenu faces as she rises through the ranks of academia and the literary world with the violence faced by Lila, even if it is, complexly, the nature of those inequities that drive wedges between women to perpetuate patriarchal power. These two truths seem irreconcilable. Lila, who for the whole of her life is surrounded by those to whom violence is not only a familiar but appropriate language, has no interest in "feminism" per se, even as her struggles for autonomy and power exemplify the (primarily Second Wave) feminist struggles Lenu begins to write about and build her career on. Lila is thrown out of a window by her father as a child, has her life threatened at the age of fifteen by Marcello Solaras should she date anyone else even though she has never consented to date Marcello to begin with, is beaten and raped by her husband Stefano, to whom she turned to "save" her from Marcello, and, when she transgresses by having an affair, she fills her notebooks with "sudden images of massacre and blood." Lenu, who reads Lila's journals from that time before throwing them into the river, goes on to say:

> She never wrote I will die murdered, but she noted local crime news, sometimes she reinvented it. In these stories of murdered women she emphasized the murderer's rage, the blood everywhere. And she added details that the newspapers didn't report: eyes dug out of their sockets, injuries caused by a knife to the throat or internal organs, the blade that pierced a breast, nipples cut off, the stomach ripped open from the bellybutton down, the blade that scraped across the genitals. It was as if she wanted to take

> the power away even from the realistic possibility of violent death by reducing it to words, to a form that could be controlled.

To be sure, Lenu hardly has an easy time of it either, exemplified most clearly by her molestation on her fifteenth birthday by a middle-aged man who has been treating her like a daughter and turns out to be a lecherous pedophile. While her own father favors her and—although corporal punishment is ubiquitous in their neighborhood, as it was in mine—has to be badgered by Lenu's mother to beat her and seems utterly unenthusiastic about the task, he does occasionally beat her nonetheless. Still, when having her own extramarital affair with Nino, the very same man Lila ran away with years earlier, Lenu has no similar fears for her life: while Pietro may have lost some face due to Lenu's adultery, he would lose far more, in his own community of well-bred intellectuals, should he run around acting like a thug about it. He is, as Lenu herself rightly judges, a "civilized" man, and after initially pitching some dramatic fits in which he does his best to convince their daughters that Lenu is abandoning them and insisting in telling them about her affair despite their young age (these, too, play depressingly similarly to scenes from my own life), Pietro soon settles into a benign quasi-amicability, albeit unsurprisingly being the one to *actually* physically abandon his children, considering two weeks, for example, far too long to keep them himself even in an emergency and relying mostly on his disdainful mother to "help" Lenu.[20]

The sexism in Lenu's world permeates every corner of her existence, but it does not manifest as a constant threat of murder. She takes it as a given that Pietro will contribute to supporting his children financially—and indeed he does. Lenu, more than she is aware, has come to expect a certain gentility and code of manners to pervade her life. Lila, meanwhile, is harassed and groped by her boss while working in a sausage factory, is involved in brutally violent clashes between fascists and communists, and in the end faces the greatest violence of all in the abduction of her young daughter, while Lenu's children scatter to study in France and the United States. In one generation, and even with the (in her view) social class setbacks of bringing her daughters back to Naples for a great chunk of their youth, Lenu has in fact raised children who will possess the same so-called "invincibility" of Mariarosa, while Lila's son Gennaro,

20. Pietro, along with Enzo, turns out to be one of the more principled men in the series, and while most men of his generation did not consider active childrearing to be a father's job, does take an increasing interest in his children as they grow older and eventually they even live with him in the United States.

despite Lila's passionate and vigilant efforts to provide him with the best possible early childhood education, fails utterly to class-jump and displays no interest in doing so, becoming the kind of middle-aged man (yet another "pleb") who frequently hits his honorary aunt, Lenu, up for money.

My own experiences of direct violence, by contrast to both Lila's and Lenu's, have been milder. My father was widely known and beloved in our neighborhood for his gentleness, and other than once threatening to spank me over some long-forgotten disobedience involving a silver mirror and then not following through, he had no role in the corporal punishment in our home growing up, while my mother—to whom I remained intensely close until her death in 2019—frequently flew off the handle and chased me around the house whacking me, sometimes holding me up in the air by one arm to do so or throwing Kleenex boxes at me in her annoyance. Once, when she had a hand injury, my mother kept a paddle in her drawer and let me know about it, so that I would be sure I could still be spanked even if her hand was out of commission. I have a memory of her sending me to get the paddle from her drawer one day, and of my dread, but no memory of her following through, which is less likely to be repression on my end and more likely to be that she did *not* follow through—my mother had a temper like a microwave during my youth, but she was not terribly consistent about the consequences she threatened.

While by the standards of my own progressive adult life and the way I've raised my own children, my mother's use of corporal punishment would be coded as dysfunctional if not downright abusive, anyone of my generation knows that this style of discipline was fairly ubiquitous at the time; surely in my neighborhood, if there were therapists and books espousing that it was wrong to hit your children, nobody knew about them. My mother was about five foot two, and although I found her efforts to physically discipline me humiliating because, like many only children, I often thought of my parents more as peers than authority figures, I can certainly attest that she never actually did any physical damage, and that in retrospect, considering that in later middle-to-old-age she lost her previously fiery temper entirely, many of her outbursts of anger in my youth had far less to do with me and more to do with her profound unhappiness in her sexless marriage to an older man who, while deeply kind and very funny, suffered lifelong physical and mental illnesses that dominated our lives, and about living in a neighborhood where she was regarded as an alien for being neither Italian nor Catholic.[21]

Outside of our apartment, violence was everywhere, but I brushed up against it mainly in peripheral ways. I was once beaten up by a neighborhood boy who was older and bigger than I, but in fairness it was I who had marched up to him and started kicking him repeatedly in the ankles, outraged that he had punched one of my male friends, and it's entirely likely that I would not have stopped my kicking until he hit me back hard enough to knock me down and deter me. Physical fights between girls were common in my neighborhood too, and I was in several as both the instigator and the attacked, usually somehow emerging victorious if a bit bloody despite my small size. I was known, in addition to being embarrassingly bookish, for having a hot temper and being a formidable debater, and though I didn't have the same level of reputation for toughness as Angie did, I'd progressed from being known as a shy crybaby in my earlier childhood to being someone who was mainly not messed with by the time I graduated from eighth grade and headed to high school—where one of the first things I did was threaten to beat up a group of three girls who were bullying

21. "The Hillbilly," one of my father's brothers called my mother, because if she was not Italian or Puerto Rican or Black or Jewish, what else could she be?

Alyssa, finding myself stunned when they backed down. As my lifelong friend and surrogate brother, Hector, would say, "You can take the girl out of the neighborhood, but you can't take the neighborhood out of the girl."

By that age of fourteen, however, I spent little time in the neighborhood anymore as—similar to Lenu—I had been admitted to a selective enrollment, college-prep high school not far from where I now live. There, as well as in college, and later when I lived in London working under the table as a bartender and maid and living in squats, I was subjected to the usual sexual boundary violations of life in the 1980s, when the term "date rape" was just being introduced into even academic vernacular and many of us wondered if this was a Real Thing or some politically correct fad that would soon be rescinded from us. But even amid rape culture and despite considerable risk-taking on my part, while I was often groped and coerced, I was never subject to the level of violent rape Lila endures almost nightly in her marriage, nor assaulted by any adult when I was a minor, like Lenu and many of my female friends both then and now. By the time I was in my early twenties and living with the man who would become my first husband, I was suffering from both the survival guilt of having gotten out of my old neighborhood when some of my old friends were dead or trapped, along with the secondary PTSD of having grown up surrounded by so much violence but always being the "lucky one" whose parents didn't beat me, whose mother didn't have unsafe men spending the night and making passes at me before I even had breasts, who lived in a home free of addictions and predators, and who had, by the sheer luck of the draw, been born with a knack for academics and had catapulted myself out of the environment of my youth, reinventing myself with the shield of both higher education and white skin.[22] When my now ex-husband had occasional fits of rage, I cannot say I was frightened or, even, categorized such displays as "violence."

In some ways, given my upbringing, I *still* find myself hesitant to label them as such, even though, as the years went

---

22. One of the lesser-discussed features of white privilege is the privilege to reinvent oneself. Although there are certainly upper echelon stratus of old money and elite-breeding privilege from which I would be excluded even now, it is fairly easy for a young adult to class jump seamlessly into the middle class even in the absence of actual money simply by getting an education, whereas obviously many people of color who similarly seek to elevate, as I did, continue to have negative class biases pushed upon them no matter how many degrees or what level of income they attain . . . or, you know, face accusations of not being citizens even if they are, in fact, the freaking President of the United States. So that both Ferrante and I are writing primarily about class coding and biases *among white people* obviously needs to be noted, as people of color often, even irrespective of economic class, deal with a more virulent classism that is driven by underlying racism.

by and we began raising children, these outbursts bothered me more than they had when it was just myself to bear witness. Of course, I didn't enjoy being sworn at and called names, particularly in front of people or in public spaces. But it was not until his anger began to manifest itself in front of our older two daughters that the fear once so elusive to me, the "tough neighborhood girl," took its grip and did not let go. But like Pietro, my ex-husband was a "civilized" man. He might throw the occasional fit, but this was, I believed, *just what men were like.*

Still, to equate my ex's rages with the violence suffered by many of my female friends, or by literary characters such as Lila and Lenu, felt an absurd false equivalency, leaving me confused by how to understand my own experience. And so, as the years wore on, and my PTSD from my old neighborhood, my survivor's guilt at getting out, and my broadening consciousness of how utterly unsuccessful I had been at "escaping the patriarchy" merely by attaining two master's degrees and writing books and having a spouse with an illustrious degree and prestigious career, all blended together to create a toxic brew of unrest, until eventually I embarked on an extramarital affair and spectacularly blew apart our family—just as both Lenu and Lila do in the Neapolitan Novels—hence creating a violence of my own.

FOUR

Daughterhood, Motherhood, Bodyhood

The first description of Lenu's mother, Immacolata Greco, occurs early in *My Brilliant Friend*, when Lenu is six years old. In the voice of the retrospective narrator, the older Lenu writes, "I wasn't agreeable to her nor was she to me." She goes on:

> Her body repulsed me, something she probably intuited. She was a dark blond, blue-eyed, voluptuous. But you never knew where her right eye was looking. Nor did her right leg work properly—she called it her damaged leg. She limped, and her step agitated me, especially at night when she couldn't sleep and walked along the hall to the kitchen . . .

Lenu also introduces her mother's unhappiness: her crushing roaches with her heel, there never being enough money, the occasional beatings by Lenu's father, whom Lenu adores even though he "could be threatening to me." The tensions between Lenu and her mother serve as storm clouds hovering over the entire Neapolitan Quartet, Lenu seemingly disgusted by everything her mother does or says and, in kind, her mother being openly critical of and harsh with her, initially opposing her studies and often accusing Lenu of thinking she is better than the rest of the family. When her parents fight, Lenu takes her father's part; when her parents, by contrast, laugh bawdily and display any open attraction and sexuality, she is (as, of course, many children are) even more repulsed by her mother than usual, as well as by the family's coarseness. Immacolata's body is a site of horror to her, and any time Lenu—who is described as being very pretty by many of the other characters, despite her feelings of inferiority to Lila—struggles with her own self-image, she immediately fears ending up like her mother: in other words, with a visible disability that in her thinking will disgust others the way her mother's body disgusts her.

While it is not my objective to discuss the HBO series, *My Brilliant Friend*, based on Ferrante's novels, it is notable that in that series, the actress cast to play Immacolata Greco, Anna Rita Vitolo, was forty-seven years old. This would absolutely "track" with viewers if they have read the books, as the casting of a middle-aged actress is certainly in keeping with the ways in which Lenu views her mother, with all the usual clichéd tropes of middle-aged invisibility and de-sexualization added to the (difficult to stomach, at times) naked ableism. I bring this up, however, as part of the overall discussion of how Ferrante treats age in the Neapolitan Novels as, in the books rather than the series, at the time of Lila's wedding (at the age of sixteen), Immacolata is thirty-five-years-old. This means that at the onset of the novel, when Lenu and Lila are six, the woman being described as so repulsive is only *twenty-five years old.*

The portrayal of Immacolata Greco casts a kind of cringe-worthy shadow over the Neapolitan Novels' feminist lens, if in ways difficult to cleanly reduce. As noted, Ferrante is not a writer of utopias, but rather of what life under the patriarchy is *actually like*, including the many ways in which women often compete with, betray, and revile one another due to the higher value placed on the male gaze and romantic love than on other qualities such as loyalty in friendship or hard work. And so, it is difficult to "fault" the young Lenu—or even the adult Lenu—for responding to her mother's body with a kind of visceral fear that she herself will be similarly afflicted, given the harsh world in which both women live. Says our narrator about her young self: "I thought that, although my legs functioned perfectly well, I ran the constant risk of becoming crippled." This even drives the origins of Lenu's friendship with Lila, who "had slender, agile legs," leading Lenu to deduce that "if I kept up with her, at her pace, my mother's limp, which had entered into my brain and wouldn't come out, would stop threatening me."

The Immacolata Greco of these early pages is only about a year older than my own eldest (twin) daughters, making it even more difficult to not read these words with a sense of fury on Immacolata's behalf. After all, here is a very young mother who, despite the climate of the late 1930s for a woman who does not meet conventional beauty standards, manages to find a respectably employed husband (Lenu's father is a porter), bears four healthy children, and continues to have an active and seemingly ribald sex life through most of the books, all while tending endlessly to the family's apartment and the needs of children and a husband. It is on the backs of her parents that Lenu ascends, as the family makes considerable sacrifices (not that Immacolata doesn't bitch about them plenty) in order to send her to school rather than having her at home helping her mother or going to work full-time to help support her family, as my own father did at the age of thirteen in Chicago, 1934, leaving the eighth grade to work in a factory, and as Lila does because her father cannot be persuaded to send her to school and throws her straight out of a window instead.

As a feminist, as a mother, as someone who grew up in a similarly economically and educationally depressed neighborhood, I find myself wanting to jump through the pages of *My Brilliant Friend* to help young Immacolata, already ancient in the eyes of her daughter while she is in fact the age of, say, the characters in the early seasons of *Friends*. One can't help but wonder where the novel about Immacolata is: the story of the woman who *doesn't* get out, doesn't ascend, who lives an "ordinary" life of poverty, sewing, cooking, cleaning, birthing children, crushing the endless roaches, screwing her husband, all in an impossibly tiny apartment, all on a leg that causes her pain, in a world where she is seen as disgusting to her own daughter, and is trauma-bonded to a man who validates her sexuality and provides her with the respectability of marriage, but beats her whenever he feels the urge? At times I feel tempted to push Lenu aside and say, *We get it, you're intelligent, you're bound for greater things, but you are not always the most interesting person in the room!*

Should I mention, here, that I, myself, limp?

Unlike Immacolata, this was not true in my youth. Until the age of forty-seven, I was able-bodied (if not always the vision of vibrant health) and, despite a lifelong distaste for team sports, generally fit, thin, the type of woman who could still do the splits to entertain my children and who did backbends in yoga classes and cartwheels on lawns. But in November 2015, in the midst of my divorce, I was diagnosed with breast cancer, and within the year I had had a bilateral mastectomy, lost my hair in chemotherapy, faced complications such as being hospitalized for neutropenia and developing lymphedema in my left arm, underwent breast reconstruction, and slowly began to realize that the hip pain I'd believed a temporary side effect of chemo was, in fact, permanent, and that all that was left of my left hip was bone-on-bone spurs. For the next two years, I limped increasingly, my range of motion dwindling such that I was unable to climb stairs and had to be dropped off in front of restaurants or literary events because I might not be able to make the walk from a parking space. My left hip was replaced in 2018, by which time my right hip had already begun its own deterioration, and despite my determination to stave off a second surgery with pilates, yoga, CBD, acupuncture, blah blah blah, and my success for more than five years, I am at the time of this writing planning for a second replacement, on the right hip.

The shame of my limp, both in its more severe form

before my first hip replacement and in its lesser incarnation now, has been . . . intense . . . in ways hard for even me to pinpoint exactly. While many might assume a bilateral mastectomy would be far more psychologically upsetting than a hip replacement, for me this has not proven true, as my mastectomy did little (beyond the first couple weeks after surgery) to change how I functioned or presented in the world. It was a private emotional loss—the loss of my nipples in particular; the loss of that erogenous zone just as I was beginning a new life with my (now) second husband—whereas my limp, my hip and leg pain and restricted movements, felt and at times *feel* like a public spectacle. My children, of course, were impacted by this change in my functioning, having to carry grocery bags and luggage up and down stairs for me, having to curtail their own gaits whenever we were out in the world at a museum, a music festival, hiking in Puerto Rico. I believe it would be fair to say I witnessed them struggling to adjust to this change and sometimes seeming viscerally annoyed with me as though I was walking so snail-like on purpose. Even that *perceived* irritation evoked shame in me, and often lingers in the back of my mind and prompts me to apologize ahead of time for ways in which I may inconvenience everyone with my slowness. *Why*? Like Immacolata, I "cannot help" my limp, and despite it I continue to lead an almost absurdly active life, working numerous jobs, traveling for work and pleasure, having an active sex life, exercising, managing a household—though thankfully *not* having to crush roaches or receive marital beatings. Still, the shame at having crossed the threshold at which *my body* has become, even slightly, a thing of revulsion to others, possibly my own children—to go from being the one who judged and reviled my own mother to being the one who was judged and reviled? Well, that shame cuts deep and is aimed mainly at my former self, not my limping self, as—like Lenu—I was once a daughter too, my mother's body a site of horror, repugnance, and fear as much as a site of nurturing, comfort, and love.

Growing up, I almost never saw my parents touch one another. Sometimes, driving in our old blue Chevy, my father would rest his arm along the bench seat and stroke my mother's hair. Even now, this memory evokes a feeling of warmth and tenderness in me—unlike Lenu, whose parents were prone to jocularly joke about their sex life in her presence, I was *desperate* for my father to show my mother any affection, and something elatedly uneasy settled in me when he did. But mostly, he did not. My father was intensely devoted to my mother—although he hung out at his men's club and sat on the porch talking with his male friends, for the most part my parents spent almost all their available time together. Like many women in my neighborhood, my mother didn't drive, and my father chauffeured her to work every morning and picked her up every day at 4:30 PM—unless he was in the hospital, I don't believe my mother ever took public transportation to work. Nor was my father ever "out late with the guys." Due to a bleeding ulcer, he did not drink, and he and my mother led a tranquil life, sitting on our couch every night watching TV or listening to jazz albums. They were both conflict-avoidant to a fault and rarely fought. But their intimacy was like that of siblings. By the time I was five, my father no longer slept in the back bedroom he and my mother once shared and took up residence on the daybed in the living room, ostensibly so that he could hear potential burglars if they tried to break in.[23] But although this was my father's party line, I felt layers

23. There was apparently a rash of burglaries in my old neighborhood a couple of years prior to my birth, and this coincided with my father's first so-called "nervous breakdown," as he became increasingly paranoid that their apartment would be targeted, layering the front door with multiple locks and becoming unable to sleep, eventually growing addicted to Valium and ending up in the psychiatric hospital after hearing voices telling him to kill himself and my mother. It is unclear whether, at the age of forty-five or so, this was his first psychotic break, or merely the first that had a witness—my mother—who found his behavior shocking

of subterfuge behind it and believed that he clung to his fear of burglary (what did we have that someone would want to steal?) to avoid my mother's potential desire for physical intimacy should they be alone in a dark room every night sharing a bed.

The layers of this potential subterfuge were complicated, presenting me with two choices, neither of which were comforting to my young mind. On the one hand, my father was "still crazy:" no one else's parents had been to a "mental hospital," and the term "nervous breakdown" was whispered when adults believed I couldn't hear. On the other hand, if I did not choose to believe my father was mentally ill, yet it was patently clear that we were not under actual threat from robbers, then he must be avoiding my mother because *something was wrong with her.* "Everyone" knew men wanted sex all the time, but my father would not sleep with my mother, would not touch her. She must be damaged, I concluded, and I—her only daughter—might be damaged, too.

When I was eighteen, I would hear my mother's version,

---

enough that he ended up seeking help. Although my father was never diagnosed with anything formal besides "depression," he had several similar psychotic breaks in my lifetime that worsened considerably with age until, by the final years of his life, he was delusional almost as frequently as he was lucid.

despite not really wanting to—she would explain that my father had always been "neurotic" about sex, initially having to get a little drunk before they got it on, but that after his breakdown in 1967, he no longer had any interest in sex with her at all. The night they conceived me was the only time that year they'd had intercourse, and once she had a child my father informed her that he wanted her to leave him alone now in that department, but that he understood she might "have needs" and so long as she didn't leave him, he would not pry or cause trouble if she took the occasional lover. My mother—thirty-five-years-old when I was born—considered his offer but never took him up on it, unable to bear the thought of hurting someone whose physical and mental health were so fragile.

As a young woman hearing this story, I believed her choice a big mistake. She had his "permission"—why should she live a life untouched? Now, having lived out the unintended consequences of having a lover outside of marriage, I understand her better, even if her choice (as evidenced by my actual life) was not the one I would have made. My mother, despite being nearly eleven years younger than my father, felt responsible for him on nearly every level spare driving the car, and she feared instigating a situation that, despite my father's assurances, could lead to the demise of their relationship. She was, she told me more than once, afraid that if they ever divorced, especially once they had me, my father might take his own life. She was the one who worked after he went on disability; she managed our household money, made all our medical appointments, did all paperwork—I never saw my father so much as write a check—and she also was the overwhelmingly primary caregiver of me and did most of the housework (notably aside from cooking!) despite being the one with the paying job. My father practiced a kind of learned helplessness in their dyad that sounded like night and day from the man he'd once been, someone who did things like drive to New York just to get a piece of proper cheesecake, who wore Zoot suits and was an unapologetic Anglophile in a neighborhood where all these things were decidedly weird. And my mother enabled his passivity, perhaps taking it as proof that he loved her even though he wouldn't touch her. In the lens of my adult mind, things look one way—but from my child-perspective, they looked like something else.

My mother was a beautiful woman in her early years with my father. He always said she looked like Isabella Rossellini, and under different circumstances I might have been one of those daughters who grew up under the shadow of a more beautiful mother, as my mother herself had been with her own glamorous mother. But as it turned out, the longer my mother went without sexual intimacy, the more weight she put on, until she eventually became what medical professionals cruelly label "morbidly obese." Decades before body positivity movements, my mother was full of self-loathing and perpetually on a diet, going to T.O.P.S., Weight Watchers, Jenny Craig when it was new (always chauffeured by my father, who would at times make jokes about my mother's weight but then in the next breath offer her ice cream . . . yes, clearly it served him well for her to be heavy, as by the standards of the time and from his own perspective, this made her less desirable to other men and allowed him to withhold affection with less chance of her leaving him). My mother spoke often about her weight loss goals, but only twice in my life did she ever lose a significant amount of weight, and both times she regained it all and more.

When I was six years old (the same age as Lenu when she is repulsed by her mother's body), my mother quit smoking and gained forty-six pounds. I began to equate my father's lack of touch to my mother's weight. By the age of seven, living with my mother's unhealthy eating habits and amid the general processed-food-1970s, especially for those like our family who existed below the poverty line, I too began to gain weight, and by the age of nine I was being teased at school, called "Hungry Hungry Hippo" for my weight and taunted with "Hee Haw!" for my overbite, even though I punched the boy who said the latter in the face hard enough to catapult him backward so that he fell over his desk. While guys fell at Angie's feet, and by ten she had a boyfriend with whom she regularly made out; while even Alyssa, who was not particularly popular, had two boys competing over her, no one wanted to date me with my chubby body, my acne, my buck teeth, my frizzy hair. How to make sense of the fact that, although I despised the guys in my neighborhood, gang members and dropouts who exuded machismo and treated girls badly as a point of pride, I was nonetheless mortified by my own lack of desirability to them? I was "like my mother," and it filled me with utter disgust.

By the summer I turned thirteen, I had an eating disorder and dropped thirty-two pounds rapidly—I would not shake disordered eating for more than a decade. Although my PTSD about the levels of violence in my neighborhood kept me fairly chaste in high school other than the occasional drunken make out session at a party, by college I was hypersexual, having one-night-stands, picking up strangers at clubs and in foreign countries, all but living in a tight black miniskirt, my hair perpetually teased, endlessly talking to my friends about the clitoris and how important it was for them to learn their bodies and understand what made them come and not to rely on men. I put on a veneer of sexual empowerment rooted in feminism, but my greatest fear in the world was that I would be desexualized like my mother—that a man I was willing to have sex with would not *want* to have sex with me. If I went a hair above 100 pounds, I immediately went on Slim Fast.

What a relief it was, truly, to meet my future (ex) husband four days after my twenty-second birthday and say goodbye to all that—to settle down and stop proving myself in the *Hunger Games* of the dating world. I felt ancient, burnt out, worn thin. He was brilliant (my number one turn-on) and steeped in respectability: a grandfather who'd been vice president of an international pharmaceutical company; a mother who attended boarding school. I loved him so much I was nearly sick with it. And: I wanted so badly for him to tell me I was beautiful, to praise my body, my face, to be besotted by my physicality, to have the kind of passion I read about in books or saw in films. But although we had frequent and mutually orgasmic sex, he was not wired that way, did not, to my recollection, use the word "beautiful" to describe me until I had already left him twenty-five years later.

Was he responsible for my insecurities, for my father's treatment of my mother, for the weight of the patriarchal gaze that sets women against ourselves in pursuit of validation we will only lose in this youth-obsessed culture when we reach a certain age anyway? Well, of course not. Would it have killed him, though, to compliment his wife's appearance? To this I can only say that he was as entitled to his demons as I was to mine, and that ours fed off one another until his tendency to withdraw and withhold and mine to chase and need finally flipped like a light switch and I checked out, stopped caring anymore what he was willing or able to give, some years before beginning my affair.

And still, my mother's body remained a site of horror to me.

She was starved for affection. I was her only child, and we were close, symbiotic, codependent in a way I still, frankly, miss like hell now that she is dead. And yet—like my ex-husband did to me in withholding compliments he must have known I craved (seeing as he did how hard I worked on my weight, my skin, my fashion choices, every aspect of my appearance), I withheld the touch I knew my mother craved, only even hugging her when it seemed absolutely essential such as when returning home from a trip. Long before the internet boasted such facts, my mother had read that people "need twelve hugs per day," and she trotted that out often in a way that made me feel pressured into contact, into meeting her needs, and inspired in me a contrary urge *not to*, in ways that will haunt me until I die. Her "neediness" repulsed me, the way she seemed to plead for affection—a situation only alleviated when I supplied her with three grandchildren to cuddle and adore. But when they, too, outgrew that sweet lap-sitting, snuggly stage, when my father died in 2015 and my mother lived alone in the downstairs apartment of my house, why for the love of god did I not walk down there and hug her twelve goddamn times per day? Or, most days, even once.

Why are we so often passive aggressively cruel to the people we love best?

Sometimes, when I am limping to the annoyance of one of my children, unable to walk fast enough, unsteady in my gait and accidentally bumping into something, I feel a certain sad satisfaction in knowing how irritated they must be by my body. I feel *close*, in such moments, to my mother, even though I do not believe in a heaven from which she would be looking down on the scene. I feel such a profound understanding of my children, too, of the myriad ways in which my body has been an affront to them—terrorizing them with my cancer, my lopped off breasts, my shredded hair, their possible fear that I had left their father only to go and die on them; embarrassing them with my wild affair with a punk rock musician with bipolar disorder and then writing a memoir about it all . . . Christ, now I am running around *limping*, too, and making my children carry things for me? Is it strange to say that perceiving their possible revulsion makes me feel as tender toward my younger, careless self as I do furious at her?

Our mother's bodies are a reflection of all our greatest fears.

Even by the third book of the Neapolitan Novels, *Those Who Leave and Those Who Stay*, Lenu remains in a state of terror around her mother's body. When she gets sciatica during pregnancy, developing a temporary limp that sends her into a tailspin, her gynecologist asks, "Why are you so worried . . . you're such a serene person." Lenu, old enough to be shamed by her own cruelty, lies, but tells the reader, "I was afraid that my mother's gait had caught up with me, that she had settled in my body, that would limp forever, like her."

In the heteronormative world, women's bodies are many things. They are objects to possess; they are sites of violence; they are a competitive sport; they are looked at, endlessly, and judged, appraised, commented upon; they are useful machines for childbearing and the feeding of children; their sexual appeal sells products and the promise of sex appeal makes them prime consumers of products; their violation serves as plot points as they are continually murdered, raped, and otherwise tortured across films and television series; they are not fit to be the president even if the alternative is a loud and proud rapist. To the very young girl, her mother's womanly body can be a site of aspiration and admiration ("Mommy, your boobies look so nice in that dress!" I remember one of my daughters joyfully proclaiming when she was four or five). But by the time most girls reach their teens, they have internalized negative messaging not only about their own bodies but about the repugnance of middle age and the asexual invisibility of mothers.

In the mother-daughter lottery, I have gotten off easy. My daughters and I share clothes and shoes; they often compliment my taste. My older two are almost supernaturally good at buying me gifts—they know precisely what I like, every nuance of my preferences, in a way no lover ever has. I was good at buying my mother gifts, too. When I was a younger adult, my taste overlapped with hers almost identically (she was a sucker for anything Victorian) before my aesthetic evolved with age. Yet I did not like the way she yawned; I did not like the way she chewed; I—more than once, far more than once—chided her for walking too slowly when we would take my young twins to the park together; oh, how absolutely insane it drove me in my youth the way she took our front steps one at a time, stepping each cautious foot onto both steps, though she was only in her late forties. Now, my children tell me I swallow too loudly, that my snoring could be mistaken for a bear. What comes around goes around.

The taboo around mothering while attempting to have a life external to the domestic realm is a constant theme in Ferrante's work, and it turns out that—as for me—what comes around goes around for Lenu, too. Sally Enrico states in her essay "An Unnatural Mother: Elena Ferrante and Motherhood," that Ferrante is "writing what most don't even admit to thinking. This is especially true regarding Ferrante's depiction of motherhood, one filled with frustration, difficult choices, and the constant threat of the loss of identity."[xi] She continues that, "Unlike most writers who take on the subject, Ferrante doesn't couch her characters' pain and confusion in self-deprecating, mommy-wants-to-crawl-into-a-wine-bottle humor."

At the same time, one of the essential truths of Ferrante's work, which is evidenced writ large in the Neapolitan Novels, is that men leave, and that fatherhood does nothing to deter them. Crushingly to Lenu, Nino ultimately follows in his womanizing father's footsteps, discarding both his lovers and his offspring like used tissues, and while he does not seem to be a rapist or pedophile like his father, he—like so many men in the Neapolitan Novels—takes up with a number of unsuitably young women. But as with violence, Nino's actions are so ubiquitous among men that they are without consequences.

For example, Lenu, having been smitten with Nino since elementary school, seems remarkably unbothered when she learns that a young activist, Silvia, has had Nino's child and promptly been left to care for the baby alone. Silvia is even younger than Lenu—who is not yet a mother—yet Lenu is initially impressed by Silvia's involvement in political rallies and her bohemian lifestyle despite having a child; she is awe-struck by Silvia's nursing her son in public while actively taking place in intellectual conversation. Later, when she and Silvia are staying in the same house, Lenu falls under the spell of baby Mirko, drawn to him with confusion, wondering if she, too, wishes for motherhood—though she characteristically asks herself, "And if my mother should emerge from my stomach just now when I think I'm safe?" When Lenu learns that Nino is the baby's father, her near-mystical fascination with Mirko begins to make sense to her, though when she asks Silvia if Nino takes an interest in the child, Silvia laughs and murmurs "bitterly," "Only the child remains, he's part of you; the father, on the other hand, was a stranger and goes back to being a stranger."

This fails to put Lenu off Nino, and even when she speaks to her future sister-in-law about the situation, the other woman merely smiles and says, "Nino is fascinating, the girls fight over him, they drag him this way and that. And these, luckily, are happy times, you take what you want, all the more since he has a power that conveys joy and the desire to act," pronouncing further that the movement needs "people like him."

At the time, both Lenu and Lila herself also believe Lila's son, Gennaro, to be Nino's, a product of their affair, and not Stefano's, Lila's husband at the time of conception. Nino has abandoned Lila, too, and Lenu fees "humiliated" for both her and Lila, concluding that "Nino was not fleeing his father out of fear of becoming like him: Nino already was his father and didn't want to admit it." Still, even after this powerful epiphany she says, "Yet I couldn't hate him."

Although the fathers Lenu and Lila grew up around beat their wives and children (and Lila has married a man who has internalized this same toxic masculinity and seems to believe Lila needs to be broken like a horse), divorce and abandonment were not a part of their girlhoods, spare Nino's married father's abandonment of his lover, Melina, who subsequently goes mad.[24] Married fathers don't go anywhere in the 1940s and 50s when Lenu and Lila are growing up, unless of course they die by murder or natural causes or are sent to prison for murder. In the new political, literary, and intellectual circles Lenu finds herself traveling in, a spirit of free love dominates, and yet it is a nascent movement that has not yet grappled with what happens when sex without marriage results in pregnancy—to the extent that anyone seems to be thinking of this at all, fathers appear almost entirely let off the hook. In the nebulous new world of the sexual revolution, one in which there is not yet a common vernacular for things like child support for an unwed mother, women—often not even out of their teens—are left to fend for themselves and their children. Lenu avoids this fate initially by marrying the respectable Pietro, with whom she has two daughters, yet Pietro proves virtually no help in childrearing, and when she ultimately leaves him for Nino, Nino predictably fails to leave his own wife and children and keeps Lenu to the side of his life. Then Pietro, likely the most conventionally "upstanding" character in the novels, casually abandons his daughters to Lenu's care almost

24. The Woman Who Goes Mad After Male Abandonment is one of the most frequent figures in Ferrante's work.

entirely, too. There are no consequences for these actions, nor is anyone particularly surprised by them. And so, the feeling of intense burden that so many of Ferrante's women experience about motherhood is inextricable from the fact that fathers who rage and hit (but try to provide financially) have now been replaced by men who (maybe) offer sexual pleasure and the rush of infatuation, but then move on with few to no strings attached. Although Lenu's own fate may not involve the squalor and violence Immocalata endured, she is in the end no less beleaguered as a mother.

Lila's feelings about pregnancy and motherhood are initially even more extreme. When pregnant for the first time, she laments to Lenu, "Men insert their thingy inside you and you become a box of flesh with a living doll inside. I've got it, it's here, and it's repulsive to me." Although Lila and Lenu both go on to be devoted to their children, it is at considerable cost to their own lives. When Lenu is pregnant for the first time herself, a thrilled expecting young mother, Lila warns her, "The life of another . . . clings to you in the womb first and then, when it finally comes out, it takes you prisoner, keeps you on a leash, you're no longer your own master." Lenu feels anger, doesn't want to listen to her friend, believes Lila is trying to drag her into her suffering, and several pages later, calls to tell Lila that giving birth to her daughter was "a wonderful experience . . . the pregnancy, the birth. Adele is beautiful, and very good." Retorts Lila, "Each of us narrates our life as it suits us."

Lenu will go on to struggle, and mightily. To be a writer and cultural critic as a young woman is rare enough at the time, but to manage it while raising three daughters (Imma, her youngest, who is by Nino, does nothing to deter his departure from Lenu's life or his continued efforts to bed Lila) is soul-crushing in the Italy of early Second Wave feminism. As Sally Errico points out:

> Lila's ability and willingness to watch Elena's children whenever she needs to work . . . enables Elena to piece together her professional success. In this sense, Lila provides Elena with a platform that the men in Elena's life cannot, or will not, though even that comes at a price: mired in her own difficulties, Lila begins to increasingly question Elena's maternal competence and willingness. Elena feels guilty—but she does not stop working. "We weren't made for children," Lila tells Elena.[xii]

But who *would* be made for children under such

circumstances? No longer working and devoting herself solely to an idyllic state of motherhood is not even an option for Lenu, a divorced woman, any more than it was an option for me some fifty years later in the United States. Like Lenu, I worked during my first marriage, but I did not *require* the income for my children's survival. Once I was parenting alone, and in my case into my second marriage, in which my husband is a professor, writer, and musician, and does not earn the kind of money that would support a wife and three children (and, for a time, my mother!), the need to continually hustle for money while somehow holding on to my own identity as a writer amplified radically. How to never allow my children to become casualties of this reality has dominated much of the past eight years of my life. But even in our current post-Dobbs and post-pussy-grabbing-president hellscape, here on the ground things *have* changed since Lenu's days of raising minor children and no one—my own children included—ever questioned whether either my desire or necessity to work rendered me not "made for children." Although many of the mothers at my children's elementary schools were stay-at-home moms, among my literary and academic friends, and certainly among other divorced mothers, those without full-time jobs—and often more than one—are far more the exception than the rule, and the stigma of what motherhood is "supposed to" look like has shifted.

Yet . . .

Well, I say this with the full awareness that for many women near the end of the first quarter of the twenty-first century, including in the United States, such stigmas remain, and the so-called "Mommy Wars" between women who stay at home vs. those who work outside the home, between those who breastfeed vs. those who use formula (and those who breastfeed but stop at a year vs. those who continue indefinitely), between those who send their children to school vs. those who homeschool or unschool, between those whose children sleep in their own beds at night vs. those who co-sleep, rage on. The persistence of judgment against mothers not only by the dominant culture at large but *by other mothers* remains as loaded a minefield of ways for women and mothers can be vilified and cast as failures as in Lenu's and Lila's time. It is only that now this fate does not befall *every* mother, whereas once the only way to avoid it was to avoid pregnancy altogether—a hard thing to achieve in a world in which husbands own their wives' bodies and birth control pills are brand new and exceedingly hard to obtain, requiring subterfuge and lies.

Yet . . .

When considering motherhood, there is also the

overwhelming matter of love.

Ferrante, who in interviews has consistently given the impression of being a mother herself, is a harsh critic of the structures motherhood imposes, but she does not forget love. Upon giving birth to her firstborn, Adele, and laying eyes upon the child, Lenu experiences a "pleasure so piercing that I still know no other pleasure that compares to it." And Lila, so irreducible in Lenu's eyes, is only finally truly broken by the abduction of her daughter Tina, such that she is never the same, and never seems to truly experience joy again. If the mother/daughter bond is a fraught one, a troubling one, it is also less breakable, more lasting than those formed with men. Ferrante wrote in 2018 that, "My mother was very beautiful and very clever, like all mammas, so I loved her and hated her." She goes on to write, "A secret cord that can't be cut binds us to the bodies of our mothers: there is no way to detach ourselves, or at least I've never managed to."[xiii] (Nor have I, Elena, nor have I . . .)

In contrasting these words to those of Silvia, the young mother of Nino's son, about men, *the father, on the other hand, was a stranger and goes back to being a stranger*, it is clear, despite any angst, bitterness, or struggle, where Ferrante believes the more primal bond for women lies.

FIVE

The Elephant (Not) in the Room: Representation, Erasure, and Authorship

Remember the bath scene?

I didn't when I re-read the Neapolitan Novels prior to writing this book, but my Facebook thread helped me to see this scene as a sort of secret entry to the map of Lenu and Lila's lives. Oh, how Lenu desires Lila in this scene! It's a desire she never feels the equal of for anyone but Nino, in a sense making his body a symbol not only of her desire for him—which has existed since childhood—but of her longing for Lila, too.

While there is no question that the Neapolitan Novels pass the Bechdel Test (if you want to listen to two teenage girls talk about all the books you only read the Cliff Notes versions of in high school, you are in the right place!), there are other common "gendered" tropes Ferrante doesn't avoid quite as fully and in fact willfully embraces and interrogates, such as the tendency to use mirroring between women protagonists to an extent that some readers have questioned whether Lenu and Lila are actually intended to be two distinct women or to represent two sides of a single woman (there are entire Reddit threads on this).

The use of "mirroring," in which two enmeshed characters (often representing dark/light or bad/good) is a highly common device employed by writers and filmmakers, often in horror, thrillers, or even black comedy: think films like *Single White Female*, *Black Swan*, and the recent Tod Haynes movie, *May December*, written by Samy Burch (she/her). This is obviously not a technique specific only to female characters—*Fight Club* pushes it to its wackiest boundaries—but I believe it would be fair to say that the trend is more common when treating female characters. I've used it myself, in writing about literal twins in my debut novel—and in my third book of fiction, *A Life in Men*—writing about a young woman who goes by the name of her dead friend and attempts to essentially live the life she imagined her friend would have lived had it not been cut short.

And yet, as the mother of twenty-three-year-old twin daughters myself, I can't help but wonder what it is that filmmakers and novelists alike seem to find so endlessly fascinating about the mirroring or twinning of female protagonists, rendering each, to some extent, only half of a whole. When even identical twins, in real life, are complicated, nuanced, fully formed individuals, what lures artists so irresistibly to the desire to portray women as so defined by *one other woman* that they would not be quite a full person without their (often opposite) reflection? Why did I buy into this trope in my own work? Why did Ferrante? What did it add and what might it subtract? Does it manifest differently in the hands of a woman writer or filmmaker compared to those of a man? Or have we all been so thoroughly trained by and indoctrinated into patriarchy that no matter what our gender identity or sexual orientation, we are all swimming in the same waters of how we conceptualize female identity? And are those waters too often shallow even when they are at their most deep?

Is it possible, I wonder, that I did not remember the "bath scene" when I first read it in 2015 because I unequivocally believed at that time that the Neapolitan Novels were written by a feminist woman—and that this scene was a claiming and owning of female desire, a perhaps autobiographical scene even, of which I, also a feminist woman in favor of women feeling the agency of their own desire, *approved*? Can the same scene be "empowering" if written by a woman and somehow "wrong" or "exploitive" if written by a man? (The answer *is* yes, isn't it?) And more to the point—for the sake of the argument that has been thrust upon us when it comes to Elena Ferrante, whether we wish for such an argument or not—let's just go ahead and speculate how we might feel about the bath scene featuring two sixteen-year-old girls if it was written *by an old man.*

I'll excuse you while you retch a little.

And yes, I know some of you are retching not even necessarily because *ewww, gross, pervert,* but because I am "going there"—I am "talking about it," when no one should. I am interrogating Ferrante's identity when why, for the love of *All the Things*, can no one on this earth be entitled to privacy and anonymity anymore?

Bear with me, please.

By now, if you're interested enough in Ferrante to be reading this book, you probably know at least some of the basic facts. In 2016, Claudio Gatti published "Elena Ferrante: An Answer?" in the *New York Review of Books*, revealing, creepily, that he had traced Ferrante's payments from her publisher to the bank account of Italian translator Anita Raja. Raja, coincidentally, is married to one of Italy's preeminent novelists, Domenico Starnone, described by Rachel Donadio in *The Atlantic* as, "Born in Naples in

1943, a working-class boy . . . Starnone is Italy's preeminent metafictional master, an heir to Italo Calvino."[xiv]

While it was hard to overlook Gatti's findings, the consensus seemed to be that the literary public very much *wished* to overlook them and saw them as a completely inappropriate invasion of Raja's privacy and right to remain anonymous. The overall journalistic tone toward Gatti was derisive to say the least. In "The 'Unmasking' of Elena Ferrante" for example, Alexandra Schwartz writes that, "Gatti seems to believe that he can obtain power over a great writer by exposing her, not for the purpose of interpretation or greater understanding but simply for the sake of being the first to do it."[xv] Schwartz seemed—judging by the amalgamated tone of pieces covering Gatti's "discovery," and perhaps even more so by how many media outlets failed to cover it at all—to speak for many when she went on to say:

> Like many—maybe most—enthusiastic Ferrante readers, I have no interest in knowing who the writer who publishes her novels under the name Elena Ferrante is. I don't care. Actually, I do care: I care about *not* finding out. There are so few avenues left, in our all-seeing, all-revealing digital world, for artistic mystery of the true kind—mystery that

> isn't concocted as a publicity play but that finds its origins in the writer's soul as a prerogative of his or her ability to create. That kind of mystery has a corresponding point in the soul of the receptive reader. To fall in love with a book, in that way that I and so many others have fallen in love with Ferrante's, is to feel a special kinship with its author, a profound sort of mutual receptivity and comprehension. The author knows nothing about you, and yet you feel that your most intimate self has been understood. The fact that Ferrante has chosen to be anonymous has become part of this contract, and has put readers and writer on a rare, equal plane. Ferrante doesn't know the details of our lives, and doesn't care to. We don't know those of hers. We meet on an imaginative neutral ground, open to all.[xvi]

And to many American readers—surprisingly many, given our culture's preoccupation with completely eradicating privacy in every arena of our lives—that was more or less the end of it.

But, for any of you who volitionally ended the story on this note, alas . . . there is more, and has been more for—at this point—nearly two decades. In 2017, Claude-Alain Roten published "Elena Ferrante is Domenico Starnone,"[25] citing investigations and studies dating back to 2006 and providing links to many attempting to prove—and to the minds of most scholars involved successfully proving—that Starnone is Ferrante. Writes Roten:

> In summary, nine approaches, very different from each other, come all to the same conclusion: the novels of Ferrante use a writing style strongly similar to that of Domenico Starnone. If one cannot exclude a common writing by the Starnone-Raja couple, the results of the nine analyzes, which together correspond to those of a meta-analysis, reveal that Domenico Starnone writes all or most of the novels signed Ferrante . . . Given the overwhelming majority of statistical results (9/9) and the scholars intuition, why do most international press articles support the hypothesis that Anita Raja is Elena Ferrante?[xvii]

25. This is the holy grail if one is seeking Ferrante's identity, and to be avoided at all cost if one is not: https://www.orphanalytics.com/en/news/1dex-ferrante-c-est-starnone.

Arjuna Tuzzi and Michele A Cortelazzo, who published "What is Elena Ferrante? A comparative analysis of a secretive bestselling Italian writer," in 2018, likewise analyzed 150 novels by forty living Italian novelists and concluded that, "Amongst the authors included, Domenico Starnone, who has been previously identified by other investigations as the possible hand behind this pen name, is the author who has written novels most similar to those of Ferrante and which, over time, has become progressively more similar."[xviii]

In the United States, however, the frenetic research of these Ferrante Unmaskers was like the proverbial tree falling (over and over again) in a forest surrounded with soundproof walls. It was not until 2021 that *Literary Hub* published "Have Italian Scholars Figured Out the Identity of Elena Ferrante? Elisa Sotgiu on Reading Gender and Class in One of the Great Literary Mysteries of Our Time,"[26] reluctantly verifying what by then numerous studies and papers in Italy, both impersonal algorithms and critical side-by-side readings of their novels, had essentially proven *to the extent that it can be proven in absence of an admission*:

26. This is one of the most essential pieces to understanding the breakdown of how Starnone was unmasked as Ferrante, and lacks the mathematical equations and science-speak contained in the actual studies themselves: https://lithub.com/have-italian-scholars-figured-out-the-identity-of-elena-ferrante.

Starnone is Ferrante.[xix]

That Raja and Starnone are married makes Gatti's original predatory sleuthing into Raja's bank accounts one more piece of evidence. And while no one can prove that Starnone and Raja are not collaborators who decided on a pen name rather than dual authorship, algorithms have shown Starnone to be the one writing the actual prose. Still, one might therefore imagine Raja to be providing much of the content—that perhaps Starnone is, with his wife's input, even telling some version of her fictionalized life story? Yet as Alexndra Schwartz states:

> The part of Gatti's claim that has unavoidable meaning for readers is that Anita Raja's biography does not at all correspond to that of Elena Ferrante as gleaned from her novels, or as described in "Frantumaglia," a work of autobiographical fragments that first appeared in Italy more than a decade ago . . . In that book, Ferrante writes that she grew up in Naples, the daughter of a local seamstress. Raja's mother . . . worked as a teacher, and was born in Worms, Germany, into a Polish Jewish family that fled to Italy in 1937. She married a Neapolitan magistrate, but the family moved to Rome, in 1956, when

> Raja was three. If Raja *is* Elena Ferrante, that would mean, among many other things, that she has no firsthand knowledge of the postwar Naples milieu that she evokes with such fiercely unsentimental strokes, the oppressive *rione* on the city's outskirts that anchors the Neapolitan novels and gives them their extraordinary texture of lived truth.[xx]

I confess that I don't want to know this. (*But . . . Elena is my friend!*) These revelations feel unwelcome, albeit I struggle to understand all the nuances of why. But one I can point to easily: that bath scene. If that scene was *not* written by a woman, can a convincing argument be made that it is not a product of the male gaze, titillated by the idea of two underage girls frolicking in a tub, one consumed by desire for the other who has goaded her into the bathing to begin with? Instead of the owning of female desire this scene would be if written by a woman, is it, rather a kind of underage lesbian fantasy of an old man? And what, even, of the designation of the ages forty-to-sixty-six as "Old Age?" If this problematic labelling came not from a woman writer who, whether we agree with her or not, experienced her own aging process that way, and instead becomes a symbol of the erasure and invisibility of women over forty by the (literal) patriarchy? What of all those wildly older men proposing to fourteen-year-old girls and the seeming absence of any young women their own ages? And what, of course, of the fact that no matter how much Lenu and Lila love each other fiercely, competition—over men, over education, over money, even over Lenu's own children—dominates their relationship, reinforcing what some on my Facebook thread complained were harmful and misogynistic stereotypes of female friendships?

As a fiction writer myself, I want these books to stand inviolate with the strong emotional response of recognition millions of women readers globally have felt upon reading them. But at times, reading the Neapolitan Novels, as well as Ferrante's other texts, with a lens of Starnone being the author, I can't shake the deep-seeded fear (the preoccupation of Ferrante's young protagonists with "becoming ugly;" the tropes of madwomen driven over the edge by male abandonment . . .) that I am being manipulated into embracing with nodding fervor the same stereotypes used to oppress women for all of time.

Or am I, if not yet the ages of Starnone or Raja, merely "getting old" to have these concerns to begin with? Can we, in 2024, still reduce gender to such stark binaries: If a man did it, it's objectification; if a woman did it, it's feminism? Is such thinking entirely passe, Second Wave nonsense? After all, I have written fiction from the points of view of numerous male characters to whom I became profoundly attached and as compelled by as my female protagonists. Shouldn't I, as a fiction writer who also once co-edited an anthology of short stories in which women authors wrote from the male point of view (about sex, no less), be the prime audience *for* fictional experimentation with understanding the psychology of the opposite sex? Or is that very question problematic, as how the utter hell can anyone "understand the opposite sex" when women, for example, constitute more than 50 percent of the human population and are the largest demographic on earth? Is there even such a thing as "female psychology," considering such vast numbers? Or is it merely that repressed people tend to be categorized by identity groups, whereas cis, straight, white men tend to be categorized as individuals?

Then there are other questions, beyond the scope of this project. How might we contextualize the debate around Ferrante's authorship, for example, within other debates around cultural appropriation in fiction, such as that around *American Dirt*[27]? If we understand gender identity to exist

27. If the reader is not familiar with the American Dirt controversy, here is a place to begin. The debate's origin is

on a spectrum, do "appropriation" arguments apply to sex in any similar way they may to race? What of the role of class appropriation, too?

What we know is that "appropriation" can be—and is—seen from more than one angle, depending on the critic. Writes Rachel Donadio in her outstandingly in-depth "Open Letter to Elena Ferrante—Whoever You Are:"

> . . . the curiosity you've aroused has also prodded me to pursue questions of a different order: about the nature of authorship, about the fluidity of personal identity, about the intermingling of life and art, about assumptions regarding gender and literary authority.[xxi]

Donadio points out that these issues of identity and literary authority are also at play in the Neapolitan novels themselves, which are constructed as "a frame within a frame." The Lenu in her late sixties writes about her friend who has gone missing as an act of both mourning and provocation. But many years prior, the younger Lenu, whose

---

largely credited to author Myriam Gurba, who discusses her original review of the novel and the larger conversation in *Vox* here: https://www.vox.com/first-person/2020/3/12/21168012/racism-american-dirt-myriam-gurba-jeanine-cummins.

proper name Elena is twinned with that of the author, also furthered her literary career by publishing a book "that drew its inspiration from something Lila had written as a girl. Elena Greco's literary career, we're led to understand, ends up crowned by the very novels we are reading. Lila inspires, Elena writes—so whose story is it?"[xxii]

It's noteworthy to point out here that such metafictional and theoretical components of the Neapolitan Novels are, as I've indicated, vastly underplayed in discussing the Ferrante landscape, and would not likely be so widely ignored among the reading public were she writing under a male pseudonym or writing, of course, *about men*. But as Donadio attests, when thinking of the Neapolitan Novels in particular, "I've come to see them as at heart an exploration of a timely and timeless theme: imaginative appropriation," inclusive of such issues as who has the authority to write about what and who—in the pages or outside them—"controls the story?" Donadio asks Ferrante (whom she has previously interviewed) directly:

> How should we readers respond to your work if we can't be certain who you are, or even whether you're a single person, either male or female? You've been heralded as an inviolable voice of womanhood, therefore understood to be one woman, and . . . I

> was in thrall to that idea myself. But wider reading since then . . . has taken me in a different direction. In choosing absence, I believe, you're challenging us to reassess the very idea of an unambiguous female authorial voice.

I still do not know quite where I stand on Ferrante and the issue of gender and appropriation. But I do know, although I have gone down the Ferrante rabbit hole largely *not wanting to know*, that pretending *not* to know is another thing entirely and precludes our being able to have vital discussions extending well beyond the case of Elena Ferrante. Is it bizarre that a casual Google search is still likely to refer to Raja as the individual who has been "outed" as Ferrante, despite the idea of Raja as the lone gun (wo)man now being a virtually impossible conclusion to draw? To me, it seems so. Even stalwart Ferrante fans with whom I spoke about this project seldom knew much about Starnone-gate. Is equating Raja with Ferrante a case of widespread literary denial, and even the insistence on Raja as an essential collaborator with Starnone a mere hypothesis of wishful thinking—if one of which I am personally fond—in order to continue to conceptualize of Ferrante as female? Here, Donadio, provides perhaps the most comprehensive context of the Raja Question:

> She hasn't published much under her own name, except for insightful introductions to works she's translated from German into Italian. But she has been particularly devoted to the work of the East German author Christa Wolf . . . In a 2015 lecture, Raja spoke about Wolf's preoccupation with "the difficulty of saying 'I,'" the challenge of capturing a story in one voice or one person . . . Wolf's 1968 novel, *The Quest for Christa T.*, which appeared from Edizioni E/O in Raja's Italian translation in 2003, is about a woman who reconstructs the life of a childhood friend after the friend goes missing. That is, of course, exactly the same frame as your Neapolitan novels . . .[xxiii]

The establishment of an intellectual and creative tie between Raja and Wolf is an extremely important clue—and perhaps our *only* such clue if Raja's bank account can also be interpreted as having held the money for her husband to help uphold his anonymity. Wolf died in 2011, and the couple posted what Donadio calls "a heartfelt tribute to her on the Edizioni E/O website," writing that every book of Wolf's that Raja translated, "became, for the two of us, the object of months of discussion—an occasion to reflect, to learn. It wasn't only literary passion . . . it was also the desire to improve our way of looking at the world, to find instructions for how to become better people. It was above all a need for an ethics, a quest for an acceptable way of living."[xxiv] Of Wolf, Raja and Starnone wrote, "She is her books, and her books are her," and Donadio attests that they were also "affected by Wolf's bond with her husband . . . a relationship that had become 'an unsurpassable model' for them, pointing the way to being a loving, collaborative, and morally engagé couple." It is on this basis that Donadio reaches the conclusion that "[w]riting as Elena Ferrante seems to me a metafictional project, a literary game of the highest order. But it's also a far-reaching exploration of what it means to write as a woman, to be perceived as a woman writer—and what expansive possibilities may emerge when our assumptions about the author's identity are subverted."

I have not read Wolf's work. But Donadio's open letter, though published several years ago, seems to have made barely a ripple in the understanding of Ferrante's authorship here in the United States. Our literary and academic communities continue collectively put their fingers in their ears chanting *La la la* whenever Starnone's name comes up. In a 2020 piece, for example, Elizabeth Berry's "Ferrante and Feminism: Women Chasing Writing Leads to Friendship and Rivalryship," states that:

> The reader knows little about Ferrante's personal background, except that she grew up in Naples, has a degree in Classics (like Elena), and wrote a column for *The Guardian.* Ferrante stands by her belief that once a book is written, there is no need for its author—reminiscent of French theorist Roland Barthes's essay "The Death of the Author" which argues for the disconnection between a literary work and its writer. Some literary circles have tried to uncover her real identity and believe Rome-based translator Anita Raja and her novelist husband Domenico Starnone are behind the pseudonym. However, other readers believe this unmasking is violating as they believe readers should respect Ferrante's decision to remain anonymous. Ferrante's anonymity is a feminist choice in itself as she associates herself and her work with women who write anonymously to avoid social biases against women authors. She also elects a female name as her pseudonym rather than a male one which inverts the patriarchal mentality that demands a female author remain invisible.[xxv]

But *can* Ferrante's anonymity be "a feminist choice" if the author behind Ferrante is a man? And again, why is the language around Ferrante's authorship utterly eschewing the virtual proof that Starnone is, at bare minimum, heavily involved?

No debate around a single (or collaboratively created) author exists in a vacuum. Therefore, rather than following the money, per se, it may be more fruitful to engage with the concepts behind the warring factions of post-structuralist vs. feminist thought surrounding this concept.[28] It is my goal—whether Ferrante's identity impacts or does not impact, depending on our interpretation, *all* her books and not only the Neapolitan Novels—to deepen our context of understanding of one of our great twenty-first century novelists, and it seems to me that Starnone, himself a metafictional writer, is *highly* engaged with these concepts in his decision to continue denying having even a hand in the Ferrante oeuvre, and yet playing with Ferrante openly in his own work.

As cited earlier, James Wood in the *New Yorker* says

28. This happens to have been one of my areas of study in my PhD program, supervised by Cris Mazza in The Program for Writers at the University of Illinois Chicago, which I completed in 2021.

that while "Ferrante may never mention Hélène Cixous or French feminist literary theory . . . her fiction is a kind of practical *écriture feminine*." And so it is, more than a matter of essentialist male/female binaries, possibly a matter of the different theoretical frameworks between feminist theory—*l'écriture feminine* in particular—and post-structuralist theory—the death of the author in particular—that forms the crux of whether we care about Ferrante's identity, and why Starnone, possibly alongside Raja, believes we should not. Therefore, let's look a bit at the essential arguments of each school of thought.

To understand the concept of a "literature of the body"—or as the French feminists have long called it, *l'ecriture feminine*—it's necessary to begin with Hélène Cixous's groundbreaking 1975 manifesto, "The Laugh of the Medusa," which called for the creation of a new "female" language as part of a revolution through writing. Cixous (and other French feminists such as Luce Irigaray) demanded not only a new female discourse but specified that this writing should come *through the body* and focus intensely on women's sexuality. In *This Sex Which Is Not One*, Irigaray explains that, "[w]oman's desire would not be expected to speak the same language as man's; woman's desire has doubtless been submerged by the logic that has dominated the West since the time of the Greeks."[xxvi] According to the proponents of *l'écriture féminine*, women need to reclaim the negative labels the patriarchy has pinned upon them, celebrating "hysterical"[29] writing in particularly. "Woman must write herself," Cixous commands, "must write about women and bring women to their writing, from which they have been driven away as violently as from their bodies." Linking body and writing intrinsically, she proclaims, "[w]riting is for you, you are for you; your body is yours, take it" and that "[b]y writing her self, woman will return to the body which has been more than confiscated from her."

Ferrante, if we can all agree on one thing, is not French. But these movements were global, from Audre Lorde's seminal "The Master's Tools Will Never Dismantle the Master's House," in the United States to the influence of Carla Lonzi in Italy. Writes Elizabeth Berry:

> Although Lonzi passed away almost three decades before the publication of *My Brilliant Friend*, her legacy is passed down through the anonymous author Elena Ferrante who has established herself

29. This rhetoric is an intentional reclaiming of the psychoanalytic diagnosis and concept of "hysteria," which destroyed the lives of countless women not only in the Victorian Era but well into the second half of the twentieth century.

> as a feminist thinker . . . The novels take place during the same decade during which Carla Lonzi, recognized as one of the founding mothers of Italian feminism, wrote on the topic of *autocoscienza*, sexual difference, and the shortcomings of gender equality. According to Claire Fontaine, Lonzi's writings "are sledgehammers for destroying the palace of culture than men build together higher and higher every day and for showing it for what it truly is: a fortress made only to exclude." Her texts, specifically *Sputiamo su Hegel* (*Let's Spit on Hegel*) and *La donna clitoridea e la donna vaginale* (*The Clitoral and Vaginal Woman*), go beyond the boundaries of patriarchal theories and propose new radical thoughts on autonomy in societal structures and sexual pleasure. [xxvii]

Indeed (forgetting Hegel for the moment), if we want to understand where *any* of these feminists got their ideas about the patriarchal linguistic exclusion of women, we don't need to look much further than psychoanalysis. For example, Lacan saw language as a symbolic order based on binary oppositions of phallus/nonphallus: a locked system to which a girl child sees her father holding the key. Similar implications abound in Freudian theory, not the least of which is his symbolic silencing of women through his rejection of patients' testimonies about their experiences with incest, instead calling these memories "fantasies" that little girls have for their fathers. In perpetuating a legacy of women's silence about sexual abuse, in psychoanalysis, women's allegations of men's trespasses against their bodies were twisted for the patriarchy's own purposes. If female desire (and abuse) was framed through a lens of little girls' alleged sexual desires for their fathers and penis envy, we can see why feminist theorists might conclude that traditional discourse does not apply to women (and, as Lorde argued, other marginalized populations).

Yet, while feminism and psychoanalysis can hardly be argued to be in sync, both are frameworks that put Body front and center as the lens for understanding everything from our interpersonal interactions to our sexuality to, as is pertinent here, our art. On the other hand, there are frameworks that have argued essentially an opposite position—and that have at times carried much greater prominence in lit crit circles—such as post-structuralism and deconstruction.

In the world of literature and literary criticism, Samuel Beckett's, "Texts for Nothing," Michel Foucault's "What Is an Author?" and Barthes' "The Death of an Author" could be understood to threaten the very foundations upon which any "body writing," certainly including *l'ecriture feminine*, is built. Indeed, while post-structuralist critics of the 1970s were busy "killing the author," and sometimes even the *subject* of the text, women writers (both white and of color, globally) were heralding the birth of a new kind of fiction centered around both celebrations of female desire *and* the darker side of women's bodily experiences, such as physical and sexual abuse. This new writing departed radically from most previous women's fiction because it placed women's bodies at the center of the narrative from the inside out rather than from the outside in. In this "literature of the body," the question of *who is speaking* remained of utmost importance. Ironically, after having been deprived of subject status for centuries, just as they began to attain it women writers were being told that it was no longer intellectually meaningful.

This debate, chronologically, just happens to also take place in our "real world," right around the time Lenu in the Neapolitan Novels is in the most crucial stages of her own literary career, and while she does not specifically engage these warring theoretical factions, one could make a convincing case that her writing, as portrayed in the novels, embodies the debate as to whether a literature of the body constitutes a seminal development of critical importance or falls into a domain regarded as less intellectually significant and even self-indulgent. Lenu's writing is candidly autobiographical, more sexually revealing than is typical of her era, and is considered groundbreaking by certain critics while distasteful and base by others; further, these opposing viewpoints also manifest in Lenu's marriage, professional relationships, and her old neighborhood.

So, we have a fictional character writing controversially feminist work in a novel by a "fictional" author whose gender technically remains a mystery. The snake, in other words, has eaten its own tail so many times that we can hardly tell the Thing from its facsimile without choking. Further, if Starnone (and Raja?) is a "death of the author" fan, what does that even really *mean* anyway?

It can all get pretty heady. For example, in his essay "What is an Author?" Michel Foucault proclaims, "[w] riting is now linked to sacrifice and to the sacrifice of life itself; it is a voluntary obliteration of the self that does not require representation in books because it takes place in the everyday existence of the writer." And: "Where a work had the duty of creating immortality, it now attains the right to kill, to become the murderer of its author"[xxviii] Foucault further questions whether who inhabits the "subject spot" in literature is important at all. Barthes, as established, also celebrates language for language's sake as liberating when, summarizing Mallarme, he says, "it is language which speaks, not the author (1)," striving "that point where language alone acts, "performs," and not "oneself (2)."[xxix]

Okay, then. In other words, the text is all that matters. Once written, the author has no more "authority" over it than any reader. The text exists on its own, open to all interpretations, language for language's sake, if you will. Or, as I have said myself in many interviews: the text is always the same, but we all read a different book depending on what we bring to the story.

But is a text having meanings outside of authorial intention, and the author not controlling textual interpretation, actually the same as killing the author entirely? I would assert that these things have little to even do with one another. But for the moment, let's focus on the perspective that the "self" who wrote the text is utterly irrelevant in all ways and that the text, in fact, at its loftiest goal, should erase the self altogether in its all-important mission of standing alone.

Clearly, writing in order to kill the self is not a popular ambition among marginalized writers—from Bob Flanagan, an S/M practitioner who was dying of Cystic Fibrosis and whose diary, *The Pain Journal*, was published after his death; to Claudia Rankine who writes of the widespread violence and microagressions to the Black body in *Citizen*; to Roxane Gay who links her experience being gang raped at twelve to her struggles with obesity in her bestselling memoir *Hunger*. Such writers—and others, ranging from Kathy Acker to Dorothy Allison to Lidia Yuknavitch to Terese Mailhot to Marguerite Duras to Pam Houston—have been much more concerned with asserting their voices that were not previously reflected in the so-called literary canon or, perhaps, even our conceptions of language, linearity, and cohesion. They are not fighting to be "killed" but, rather, for their right to exist in the first place.

According to Jan Montefiore, author of *Feminism and Poetry*, "[f]eminists rightly attach extreme importance to the articulation of one's experience, which can't be thought and therefore in a sense doesn't exist unless it can be named and articulated."[xxx] This implies that the writing can in fact *give* experiences meaning or definition, rather than only *represent* experiences in an inadequate way. Such reasoning is obviously incompatible with post-structuralist thought, in which *naming* itself is a problematic chain of events through which signifiers are attached to the signified, all things being identifiable through what they are *not*, and no meanings being unified and fixed.

While it may be giving Gatti too much credit (and

I'm certainly not positing his motivations as feminist!), Donadio interestingly circles Gatti's sleuthing around back to this precise central schism between the two theoretical frameworks:

> Here was a hard-nosed reporter's take on a long-running, often aridly theoretical literary debate about authorship, akin to Gatti's saying, "What do you mean 'Is the author dead?' or 'Is the author a social construct?' Forget it! The author is the one who gets the royalty checks!"

What, then, of Ferrante, who—irrespective of the author's gender, is widely considered a feminist writer and has been credited as being in the tradition of *l'ecriture feminine*, and yet also seems to be playing with identity as a kind of performance art or a thing in need of obliteration? Ferrante has been cited many times talking about her affinity for *Madame Bovary*, evoking Flaubert's infamous, "*Madame Bovary, c'est moi*" in a way that might indicate not prioritizing issues such as gender appropriation. She also, however, at times downplays the role of any single author or consciousness entirely, having said to Donadio that "there is no work that is not the fruit of tradition, of many skills, of a sort of collective intelligence," and that readers "wrongly diminish the role played by this collective intelligence" when the focus is on an author as a "concrete, definite individual." This seems to be a tacit admission that Ferrante is not the product of a "concrete, definite individual." Which potentially raises complex feelings in many women readers. It is not only the identification felt with Ferrante's characters but the construct of Ferrante herself that is at stake. There can be a sense of personal betrayal when an author with whom one has the kind of personal affinity to which Messud alluded somehow transforms into an artistic "experiment" a heteronormative married couple thought up one night, maybe when talking about Wolf, and then tested—the husband with pen in hand—on readers.

Given the historical context of the debates about relevance of authorship, to conclude that Ferrante's identity simply does not merit discussion is both a highly valid perspective on the individual's right to privacy and the freedom from Gatti's grubby hands in their bank accounts, but it is also to, in a sense, fall down on the side of the theoretical debate *not* aligned with the very feminist perspective many are using, when asserting anonymity to be a feminist act on Ferrante's part, to dismiss the discussion as not worth having.

I don't fall in line with this dismissal, based largely

on the fact that Ferrante herself seems to have so much to say on these matters. Albeit she's slippery. She has openly expressed sympathy for how annoyed Starnone must be with everyone haranguing him about being her and also expresses in *Frantumaglia: A Writer's Journey*, that "A good writer, male or female can imitate the two sexes with equal effectiveness." She even quarrels with the concept of "female writing" and gender itself, in an interview with the *Los Angeles Times*:

> Certainly, female writing exists, but mainly because even writing is powerfully conditioned by the historical-cultural construction that is gender. That said, gender has an increasingly wide mesh, its rules have been relaxed, and it is more and more difficult to reconstruct what has influenced and formed us as writers. For example, I learned from the books I loved and studied, by male and female authors, and I could easily name them, but I've also been deeply affected by sentences whose provenance I no longer remember, whether it was male or female. The literary apprentice, in short, passes through channels that are hard to identify. So I would avoid saying that I was formed by this or that author. Above all,

> I would avoid saying that I was formed essentially by women's writing . . . [w]e are in a period of great change, and the presentation of gender is at risk of being not only unconvincing but not really valid.[xxxi]

Yet, ever a contrarian, she also said in an interview with *Vanity Fair* in 2015, that women "know everything about the male symbol system," but men "for the most part, know nothing about ours, above all about how it has been restructured by the blows the world has dealt us." Hence, how can a male writer, by Ferrante's own (very *l'ecriture feminine*) sensibilities, write from the symbolic system of women?[30] In this sense, by speaking as more than merely a pseudonymous author of novels about women (which I would strongly argue any author should be able to write, irrespective of gender, without intrusions from the outside world attempting to uncover their identities like they have

30. In another possible contradiction, Ferrante is, across all of her work, also a frequent utilizer of symbols, many of which—like dolls, like abandoned madwomen, like bracelets—appear in more than one of her novels. A careful reading of Ferrante's use of symbolic objects might conclude that these symbols are almost "trying too hard" to be feminine. Or, by contrast, one might conclude that such objects had significance in the lived life of the individual(s) behind Ferrante's texts. In other words, all signs point to two possible doors.

committed a crime), Ferrante has posited herself as a public figure with a loose biography, and asserted contradictory philosophical opinions as to whether it is, in effect, *possible* for her to actually be a man. Despite often stating that the purpose of her pseudonym has been to protect her privacy, she has not retreated to enjoy said anonymity but instead has turned it into a type of performance art that, as the Cuban author and historic art conservationist Rosa Lowinger recently remarked to me when we were discussing this book, calls to mind JT LeRoy. At first, I protested: Ferrante is not hiring people of another race or gender to play her at public events! But the more I consider the wide body of Ferrante's commentaries on gender, on motherhood, on "the symbolic system of women," the more I see that if indeed Starnone *is* Ferrante, the similarities may not be total, but nor are they utterly insignificant. And so we end up in a damned-if-we-do (are we harassing a woman writer who only wanted to be left in peace, knowing what the public eye so often does to women) and damned-if-we-don't (are we all putting our fingers in our ears and saying "La la la" while an old Italian man makes pronouncements on what it feels like to give birth or whether men "know nothing about" a symbolic order she calls *ours*, as women?

The few critics paying attention to whether

Ferrante-as-woman may be a metafictional construct find other traces of evidence, too, of her lure toward anonymity in art. In "The Only True Name: Who Is Elena Ferrante?" Pierce Alquist writes:

> I was particularly struck by her musings in an article for the *Guardian*[31] about a painting in the Pio Monte della Misericordia, in Naples. The 17th century painting that has captured Ferrante's attention is of a nun, "with hands joined, eyes closed and an ecstatic expression." The painting is by an unknown artist, and Ferrante writes that ever since she was a young person, she liked the term *unknown*. Not knowing the artist liberates her from thinking about the artist and gives her space to concentrate only on the art. She goes on to add that the artist while unknown to her in name, is in reality a figure she knows intimately through their art, their "only true name." It's a stunning statement, that seems to capture so much of what Ferrante is doing with her own work.[xxxii]

---

31. https://www.theguardian.com/lifeandstyle/2018/apr/07/elena-ferrante-ever-since-adolescence-i-have-liked-the-term-unknown.

Alquist goes on to postulate, then, "It would not be a pseudonym, that is, a false name; it would be the only true name used to identify her imaginative power, her ability. Every other label would be problematic, would bring into the work precisely that which has been kept out of it, so that it would stay afloat in the great river of forms."

River of Forms? That's sounding pretty damn Death of the Author to me.

But is Alquist just looking for breadcrumbs? I mean, if every single thing we ever said could be used to pore over for evidence to support a particular conclusion, might not a whole lot of false causalities—and conclusions themselves—be drawn? And how does Ferrante feel about conclusions being drawn? Is it a violation, or just part of the game? After all, I can't help but ask myself, *If someone is trying to remain anonymous, why are they publishing entire books of their letters, writing a column for the* Guardian, *and giving interviews in which they reveal (often contradictory) tidbits of their identity*[32] *to begin with?*

---

32. Among these include Ferrante often beginning interview answers with some variation on "as a girl," referring to her first pregnancy as "an anxious mental struggle," referencing two daughters and at least one grandchild, attesting to having grown up in Naples, and stating that she took care of her newborn with little assistance or money, among other autobiographical snippets.

Many of Starnone's novels have not yet been translated into English, and I will not now attempt to do an in-depth compare and contrast of those few I have read with Ferrante's body of work. But there certainly seems a strong argument for bringing all Starnone's work into English and letting the literary critics go to town. For if all of literature is an ongoing cultural conversation between writers living and dead, then might not Ferrante's conversations with *herself* be relevant fodder not just for a better understanding of her work, but for an advancement of theoretical debates around authorial identity, textual sovereignty, and identity appropriation that have been raging now for more than half a century?

It might also be . . . pretty fun. For example, in Starnone's 2021's *Autobiografia Erotica di Aristide Gambía* (which has not been translated into English), Elena Ferrante appears as a character. The novel is also, says Donadio, "a dizzying meditation on whether men can convincingly write about women and women about men," a question to which Donadio ultimately concludes, "Questioning reflexive notions about male and female writing seems to be at the core of a collaborative enterprise that, if I've understood you, expands the authority of the woman writer in fascinating new ways." Or, as Karen Bojar writes in her review of Starnone's novel *Ties*:

> But in the last analysis does authorship of the Neapolitan Quartet matter? The books have not changed. But will we read them differently knowing that the author is not a woman whose perspective has been shaped by her own experience of extreme poverty, of class and gender discrimination? Will we read the books differently if we learn that Starnone is Raja's collaborator or if he turns out to be the principal author? In my recent re-reading of the Neapolitan Quartet, I forgot all about Raja, Starnone and Gatti and became once gain totally immersed in the world of Lila and Elena.[xxxiii]

With which, in the final analysis, I find myself agreeing, even challenging myself on The Bath Scene. After all, the Neapolitan Novels may be Lenu's "memoirs," but they have never been marketed as Ferrante's! They are *fiction*, and whether written by Raja, Starnone, the pair of them, or some yet unmasked author or collection of authors, the male gaze exists in all writers—and people—schooled in what Ferrante referred to as "the male symbolic system." We also know, through the works of many feminist authors from Acker to Allison to Duras, that the male gaze can exist simultaneously with the agency of female desire—in The Bath Scene as throughout the Neapolitan novels, just as it does, of course, in life. We are all, across the gender spectrum, subject to the same upbringing entrenched in patriarchy. This does not mean that the only way a man can think of female sexuality is through prurient objectification, nor does it mean that we as women are immune from turning the male gaze on other women and ourselves, even though we are also capable of a glorious autonomy.

To this end, and during my years of reading Ferrante, my own concepts of gender have been challenged in fascinating and ultimately productive and transformative ways. While my thinking has advanced with the times in terms of cultural appropriation and the importance of the #ownvoices movement,[33] I have also grown ever more skeptical of the increased focus on "celebrity" in the arts: on influencer culture and decades of highly curated, scripted, and unreal "reality" shows and—even as the author of a memoir myself—the seemingly endless preference for "true stories" such that even when writers are promoting *novels*, we are often urged to find connections between these fictional texts and our lives and write essays about these overlaps,

33. Having graduated from college in 1990 and attended graduate school in the mid-to-late 90s, these concepts were certainly part of the cultural discussion, but they have evolved significantly since then for the better.

as though encouraging readers to buy fiction based on the author's "brand" and personal history is a given necessity.

And so, a large part of me feels that even if Starnone/Raja/whomever have taken a keen interest in the "performance" of Elena Ferrante through interviews, books of emails and letters, a column in a major paper, I find myself resisting. Yes, it would be fascinating—as some of the critics I've mentioned here have already started to do—to have the body of Starnone's work in English to read side-by-side with Ferrante's oeuvre, but that is the work of literary critics and scholars. What of *readers*? Do we need to understand the first thing about Ferrante's performance of identity in order to devour and relate to her novels, or the Neapolitan Quartet specifically? Clearly, as millions of readers worldwide have proven, myself included, the answer is no. And so, for my belief that scholars should be permitted to follow the trail without being seen as antifeminist vipers (so long as, unlike Gatti, they are not trolling anyone's bank records and are simply looking at the texts), I also in the end come down on the side of the reader's right not to give a fig who Elena Ferrante is . . . and in fact even the critic or scholar's right to disregard the performance art side of Ferrante's identity as a type of noise we are, even here in 2024, allowed to turn way down and stay on the pages of the novels, judging them based on our own subjective response to them and not any other means.

The version of myself who first read Ferrante was in my final year of a highly traditional marriage, in which we were raising three children we then believed to be cis-gendered. In the ensuing years, however, there has been a decided queering of my household. In the wake of my "Ferrante years," my youngest child came out as a trans, and, now in my second marriage, other members of our five-person nuclear family also exist on a continuum of queerness. When I look back at the 2014 Me, on holiday in Hawaii with my first husband and three pre-sexualized children, one of whom then went by different pronouns and a different name, I understand that version of *myself* as having had little more understanding than Lenu when it came to potential roles for women as wives, mothers, lovers, or, most pertinently to this text, *writers.* That former self often believed that it was my ex-husband's successful (and masculinely coded) career and income that *allowed* me to write, that made my literary lifestyle possible. We joked, both between us, and I, separately from him, that he was my "patron." Without downplaying either the privilege it is to be supported financially or how encouraging my first husband was about my writing overall in those years, this construct also sometimes served to relegate my writing not only to the arena of a "hobby," but perpetuated my own belief that my identity as a writer was inextricable from my identity as a particular man's wife, similarly, if less extremely, to the ways in which Lenu believes she requires her husband's family—the venerable Airotas—and often Nino and his reputation and connections to validate her intellectual and literary identity. As it turns out, Lenu leaves Pietro Airota and later is slowly and painstakingly abandoned by Nino until she can take no more, ending up single for the remainder of the Neapolitan Novels, raising three children with only other women for help, and, as we learn, continuing—did the reader have any doubt?—to write.

In her early sixties—a decade I myself will be but four years away from the month this book comes out—after a period of struggle and growing obscurity and thrashing against her aging process, Lenu writes *A Friendship*, a book that catapults her back into the public eye and relative fame. She did not need the Airotas, nor Nino, nor—it turns out—even Lila, as the two have long since drifted far apart, although Lila is, as ever, the muse of whom Lenu will not let go. If the great explicit tragedy of the Neapolitan Novels is the devastating and forever-unsolved abduction of

Lila's daughter Tina, its quieter tragedy is that Lenu never seems to fully embrace her own agency and autonomy: she performs for Lila until the very end, saying in the Epilogue of the quartet as she frantically scans the document of her memoir for traces of Lila, "Unless, by imagining what she would write and how, I am no longer able to distinguish what's mine and what's hers."

We are shaped by others, and so many of them disappear. Our brains are ghost houses of both inspiration and haunting. My current life bears little in common with the life I wore when I first read Ferrante (even though I am still a woman, still a wife/mother/ lover/writer, still living in a world arguably even more deeply entrenched in misogyny than in 2014 or in my childhood alongside Alyssa and Angie), and like Lenu, I often struggle with what to keep and what to let slide away. In this way as much as any identification with Lenu's old neighborhood, I "relate to her" (no matter the gender of her creator), but I also hope to learn from her mistakes and not hold on so tightly to the past that I am strangled by it.

Angie—though I certainly hope to see her again in this lifetime—is gone. This will be the third book I have published since I abandoned the concept of somehow requiring "patronage," and—now married to another writer/musician/

professor—I not only continue to write and mother but am also the primary earner in my household. If at times this is a stressor, it is also freedom. The current iteration of my family has uncoiled me from gender-role binaries I always found ill-fitting, constraining, and unfulfilling, even if I did not contain—for all my reading of gender theory—quite a language to express it for decades. Because, of course, while it may be true that a thing cannot be quite "real" if it does not have a name, it is even more true that we cannot name a thing unless it exists in some lived and experienced manifestation.

My manifestations have changed, and with them the names of things. And with that, also, Ferrante and the Neapolitan Novels. The text is the same, but the text is also never the same. I am now a different reader.

NOTES

i. O'Rourke, Meghan.,"Elena Ferrante: The Global Literary Sensation Nobody Knows," *The Guardian*, October 31, 2014, https://www.theguardian.com/books/2014/oct/31/elena-ferrante-literary-sensation-nobody-knows.

ii. Wood, James, 2013, "The Fiction of Elena Ferrante," *The New Yorker*, January 14, 2013, https://www.newyorker.com/magazine/2013/01/21/women-on-the-verge.

iii. Ibid.

iv. O'Rourke.

v. Lowry, Elizabeth, "Friends and Other Enemies," *Wall Street Journal*, November 20, 2015, https://www.wsj.com/articles/friends-and-other-enemies-1448054911.

vi. Quart, Alissa, "Why Doesn't America Have an Elena Ferrante?" *BuzzFeed*, November 10, 2015, https://www.buzzfeed.com/alissaquart/elena-ferrante.

vii. Messud, Claire, "Elena Ferrante's Neapolitan Quartet," *Financial Times*, August 28, 2015, http://elenaferrante.com/reviews/financial-times-2.

viii. "A Matter of Term—Realism, Naturalism, Hyperrealism,

Surrealism | Learn to Draw and Paint in the Academy of Fine Art Germany," Academy of Fine Art, July 1, 2022, https://academy-of-fine-art.com/en/2022/07/01/a-matter-of-term-realism-naturalism-hyperrealism-surrealism.

ix. Ibid.

x. Wood.

xi. Errico, Sally, "An Unnatural Mother: Elena Ferrante and Motherhood," *The Rumpus*, January 15, 2015, https://therumpus.net/2015/11/22/an-unusual-mother-elena-ferrante-and-motherhood/.

xii. Ibid.

xiii. Ferrante, Elena, "Elena Ferrante: 'One Morning I Looked at Myself in the Mirror and Recognised My Mother,'" *The Guardian*, August 25, 2018, https://www.theguardian.com/lifeandstyle/2018/aug/25/elena-ferrante-one-morning-i-looked-at-myself-in-the-mirror-and-recognised-my-mother.

xiv. Donadio, Rachel, "Elena Ferrante: Who Is Behind the Pseudonym?," *The Atlantic*, December 18, 2019, https://www.theatlantic.com/magazine/archive/2018/12/elena-ferrante-pseudonym/573952.

xv. Schwartz, Alexandra, "The 'Unmasking' of Elena Ferrante," *The New Yorker*, October 3, 2016, https://www.newyorker.com/culture/cultural-comment/the-unmasking-of-elena-ferrante.

xvi. Ibid.

xvii. "Elena Ferrante Is Domenico Starnone," *OrphAnalytics SA*, October 31, 2017, https://www.orphanalytics.com/en/news/1dex-ferrante-c-est-starnone.

xviii. Tuzzi, Arjuna, and Michele A. Cortelazzo, "What Is Elena Ferrante? A Comparative Analysis of a Secretive Bestselling Italian Writer," *Digital Scholarship in the Humanities* 33, no. 3 (2018): 685–702. https://doi.org/10.1093/llc/fqx066.

xix. Elisa Sotgiu. "Have Italian Scholars Figured Out the Identity of Elena Ferrante?," *Literary Hub*, April 20, 2021, https://lithub.com/have-italian-scholars-figured-out-the-identity-of-elena-ferrante.

xx. Ibid, Schwartz.

xxi. Ibid, Donadio.

xxii. Ibid, Donadio.

xxiii. Ibid, Donadio.

xxiv. Ibid, Donadio.

xxv. Berry, Elizabeth, "Ferrante and Feminism: Women Chasing Writing Leads to Friendship and Rivalryship," CISLA Senior Integrative Projects, 27. 2020, https://digitalcommons.conncoll.edu/cgi/viewcontent.cgi?article=1018&context=sip.

xxvi. Luce Irigaray, *This Sex Which Is Not One* (New York: Cornell University Press, 1985): 25. http://www.columbia.edu/itc/architecture/ockman/pdfs/feminism/Irigaray.pdf

xxvii. Ibid, Berry.

xxviii. Michel Foucault, "What is an Author?" https://tinyurl.com/33dhtfcb.

xxix. Roland Barthes, "Death of An Author," http://courses.washington.edu/smithint/barthes.pdf.

xxx. "Jan Montefiore, "The Lips that Never Lie: Female Language and Imaginary Identity," *Feminism and Poetry* (London: Pandora Press 1987), 167.

xxxi. Jacob, Didier, "In a Rare Interview, Elena Ferrante Describes the Writing Process Behind the Neapolitan Novels," *Los Angeles Times*, May 17, 2018, https://www.latimes.com/books/la-ca-jc-elena-ferrante-interview-20180517-htmlstory.html.

xxxii. Alquist, Pierce, "The Only True Name: Who Is Elena Ferrante?," *Book Riot*, December 26, 2021, https://bookriot.com/who-is-elena-ferrante.

xxxiii. Bojar, Karen, "*Ties*—A Powerful Novel by Domenico Starnone (AKA Elena Ferrante) Now in English Translation," *The Next Stage*, March 9, 2017, http://www.the-next-stage.com/2017/03/laces-powerful-novel-by-domenico.html.

OTHER BOOKMARKED TITLES

James Baldwin's *Another Country*
by Kim McLarin

William Stoner and the Battle for the Inner Life
by Steve Almond

George Eliot's *Middlemarch*
by Pamela Erens

Virginia Woolf's *Mrs. Dalloway*
by Robin Black

Christina Stead's *The Man Who Loved Children*
by Lucy Ferriss

Vladimir Nabokov's *Speak, Memory*
by Sven Birkerts

Heaven, Hell and Paradise Lost
by Ed Simon

Raymond Carver's *What We Talk About When We Talk About Love*
by Brian Evenson

Larry McMurtry's *The Last Picture Show*
by Steve Yarbrough

(For a complete series list, go to https://www.igpub.com/category/titles/bookmarked/)

Printed in the USA
CPSIA information can be obtained
at www.ICGtesting.com
JSHW080230300524
63970JS00003B/3

9 781632 461629